THE LANDLORD'S FRIEND

THE LANDLORD'S FRIEND

LANDLORDING ADVICE FROM PEOPLE WHO SEE THE PAIN WHEN IT ALL GOES WRONG

PAUL SHAMPLINA
KATE FAULKNER

Designs on Property Ltd

This book is not intended to provide personalised legal, financial or investment advice. Readers should seek professional advice with regard to such matters as interpretation of the law, proper accounting procedures, financial planning and tax before proceeding with any property investments. The authors and the publisher specifically disclaim any liability, loss or risk which is incurred as a consequence, directly or indirectly, of the use and application of any contents of this work.

ISBN: 978-178456-158-1

First published in England in 2014 by Designs on Property Ltd

Copyright © 2018 by Paul Shamplina and Kate Faulkner

The right of Paul Shamplina and Kate Faulkner to be identified as the authors of this work has been asserted by her in accordance with the Copyright, Designs and Patents Act, 1988.

The content of this book relate to laws of England and Wales.

An environmentally friendly book printed and bound in England by
www.printondemand-worldwide.com

This book is made entirely of chain-of-custody materials

CONTENTS

ABOUT THE AUTHORS

PAUL SHAMPLINA

Paul Shamplina has spent more than 25 years helping landlords with problem tenants. His expertise in lettings management and tenant evictions is second to none within the industry. Landlord Action, the company Paul founded in 1999, is widely considered the UK's leading provider of buy-to-let legal services.

Paul left school at 16 with no formal qualifications. His career in property began during the recession of the late 80s, when he worked as an outdoor clerk for a law firm in Brighton. By the age of 17, he was conducting up to 16 mortgage repossession hearings in one day at court.

He later moved back to London, where he worked for a law firm, gaining experience in all areas of landlord-tenant litigation. By the mid-nineties he had decided he wanted to work for himself and became a certified bailiff, private investigator, process server, debt collector and tracing agent, helping landlords with tenant evictions. He rented out his first property in 1997.

In 1999, having become frustrated with the high fee schedules that solicitors were applying to landlords, he founded Landlord Action with a business partner. It was the first company to offer free advice to landlords and fixed fees for evicting problem tenants.

To date, Landlord Action has handled more than 35,000 instructions. Paul has earned a reputation as the landlord's friend and campaigns regularly for landlord's rights. In 2014, Landlord Action acquired an alternative business status and, regulated by the Solicitors Regulation Authority, now issues its own claims at court for landlords. In 2017, Landlord Action was acquired by Hamilton Fraser, which owns Total Landlord Insurance, The Property Redress Scheme and Client Money Protect, and co-owns MyDeposits with the National Landlords Association. Paul remained as a director of Landlord Action, and is now brand ambassador for the Hamilton Fraser Group.

Paul has delivered more than 500 educational seminars and workshops for landlords and letting agents, helping them to understand and overcome the challenges of the property industry.

A down-to-earth Londoner with a great sense of humour, Paul has been the media's go-to person for comment and advice on landlord issues and private rented sector as a whole for many years.

Best known for the hit Channel 5 series, Nightmare Tenants, Slum Landlords, now rebranded for the fourth series as Bad Tenants, Rogue Landlords, he has appeared in numerous other television programmes including The One Show, Inside Out, BBC Breakfast, News 24, Meet the Landlord and War at the Door for the BBC; Tenants From Hell and Nightmare Tenants for ITV; as well as Channel 5 News, Sky News, CNN and on Channel 4.

He also takes part in radio phone-ins around the country, co-hosted The Property Hour on LBC with Clive Bull, and appears regularly in the press. Landlord Action's success stories have featured in trade and national press including The Times and The Daily Mail, The Sun, The Daily Mirror and in 2012 Paul was named in the top 25 most influential property people by the Daily Telegraph.

Paul worked on advising what is now the Ministry of Housing, Communities & Local Government (MHCLG) in relation to the Deregulation Act 2015 and gave evidence at Parliament relating to retaliation eviction. He also sits on the Advisory Council for The Property Redress Scheme.

He is married to Rita and has two children, Rocco and Serenna, and a pet dog, a Cockapoo called Keeco. He loves playing football and watching his beloved Spurs, and also takes part in boxing matches for charity. Each year he organises a charity event for the property industry called Rumble with the Agents. You can find out more at www.rumblewiththeagents.co.uk

KATE FAULKNER

Kate Faulkner is one of the UK's leading independent property experts. As a market analyst and industry consultant, Kate advises professional bodies, government and works with many leading property companies, including agents, developers, mortgage, insurance, proptech and various industry bodies to help them improve their consumer offering.

Since the early 1990s, Kate has bought, sold and rented 13 times and combines her passion for property with an extensive sales and marketing background. She has degrees in Economics and Marketing, plus an MBA, and worked for a number of years for Blue Chips, such as Unilever, leading sales and marketing initiatives. She is a member of the Institute of Directors, the Chartered Institute of Marketing and Society of Authors.

As a consultant to the property industry, Kate has introduced new online products; prepared for launch the National Self Build and Renovation Centre in Swindon; worked with developers to carry out part-exchange services, and consulted in the renting and letting/property investment sector. Kate regularly summarises what's happening to property prices and rents and the impact on consumers – and the industry.

To enhance industry engagement with consumers Kate helps to run The Lettings Industry Council and Home Buying and Selling Group working with forward-thinking companies and organisations to improve quality and service. Recently the TDS Charitable Foundation funded Kate and her team to produce independent research papers on the Private Rented Sector: www.propertychecklists.co.uk/categories/tenancy-deposit-scheme-reports

Kate's own business provides consumers with independent, up-to-date advice on how to buy, sell, rent, invest, renovate, maintain or build a property via a free service called Propertychecklists.co.uk and has produced the UK's only online Buy to Let TV show (www.propertychecklists.co.uk/articles/the-buy-to-let-show) along with comprehensive 'how to' guides. She has already written more than 10 property books, including four for the consumer organisation Which?: 'Buy, Sell and Move House', 'Renting and Letting', 'Develop your Property' and 'Property Investment Handbook'.

Kate presents regularly at seminars across the UK, to landlords, investors and first-time buyers, and hosts and speaks at industry conferences and chairs debates. Kate's media appearances have included BBC Breakfast News, Your Money, ITV's This Morning, BBC Radio 4's You and Yours and The Big Questions. She is a regular co-host of LBC's The Property Hour and one of BBC 5Live's midnight experts. She features regularly in local and national newspapers and magazines.

PART ONE

PREPARING FOR SUCCESSFUL LETTING

CHAPTER 1
IS BUY-TO-LET RIGHT FOR ME?

"Real estate cannot be lost or stolen, nor can it be carried away. Purchased with common sense, paid for in full, and managed with reasonable care, it is about the safest investment in the world."
Franklin D. Roosevelt

The global property industry has changed dramatically since former US President, Franklin D. Roosevelt, made that statement. In a post-credit crunch world, is his advice still valid?

These days, for investors to successfully navigate the buy-to-let market, a level of skill is definitely required. And not everyone will have the discipline to learn these skills. Consequently, contrary to what we are told in the press and all of the glossy sales brochures, buy-to-let is not an industry that everyone can – or should – get into.

But, other than 'paid for in full', the essence of what Roosevelt says about property is still valid, especially about it being 'managed with reasonable care'. As you will learn from reading this book, that can make the difference between a profitable buy-to-let investment and potentially having your property repossessed or, worse still, becoming bankrupt.

Fortunately, with effort and discipline, the skills needed to succeed in buy-to-let can be learnt. Reading this book will give you a solid foundation in the basics but it is by no means exhaustive and you should continually check the decisions you make with professionals, such as estate and lettings agents, mortgage brokers, legal buy-to-let specialists and conveyancers.

You should also – and this is the part that too many investors disregard – have a wealth management or financial investment team that includes tax and inheritance-planning specialists. It's one thing creating wealth; it's another thing retaining it.

Before you start, three key questions to ask yourself

1. What are my investment objectives?

Are you looking for an investment that will be held over the short, medium or long term? Buy-to-let is a long-term investment (typically 15 to 20 years). Furthermore, property is an illiquid asset, which means, unlike shares or bonds, your capital will be tied up in the property until you re-finance it to release some equity or sell. So if you need financial flexibility and would worry about not being able to quickly access your capital, buy-to-let is probably not right for you.

Listing your financial objectives will help to prioritise what sort of investments would be appropriate for you.

2. Do I have the capital?

The days of 'no money down' property investing are gone. Lenders are now demanding that property investments have a substantial chunk of equity and the upshot is that you are now likely to need a minimum deposit of 25%. You should also be aware that many lenders will also require proof of your own, personal income and may refuse to lend if your earnings are less than £25k. They may also refuse to lend if you are under 25 or over 75.

New rules enforced by the Prudential Regulation Authority (PRA) mean if you are building a portfolio, lenders will ask you to provide a business plan for your property investment, to show you are clear on your goals and prepared for any financial challenges you may face.

On top of this, you will need access to spare capital during your property ownership to support additional costs, for example, void periods, where the property is not being rented out to a tenant. In these circumstances, you have to continue financing the mortgage and any bills yourself.

It's highly likely that, at some point, you'll get problem tenants who will refuse to pay rent; this was the very reason I founded Landlord Action. I spend my days dealing with tenants who won't pay and won't leave. And although that's not the landlord's fault, the lenders still expect mortgage payments to be made!

Remember that the property will also need periodical refurbishment, in addition to ongoing maintenance.

Do you have sufficient capital reserves to cover yourself in these scenarios?

3. **How involved do I want to be?**
    Are you a hands-on or a hands-off investor? Do you have the resources to manage the property? Do you have the expertise? Do you have the time?

    Letting property has changed significantly in recent years, to provide safer housing for tenants. New rules introduced in April 2017 mean councils are now much stricter and can fine landlords up to £30,000 for failing to comply with rules and regulations such as those set out in the Housing Health and Safety Rating System (HHSRS).

    Although there are plenty of management agents out there who can manage the property (for a fee, of course), you're likely to need to be involved at certain points. For example, when taking Court action against a tenant, I always recommend (where possible) that you, the landlord, attend Court and engage in the proceedings yourself.

If you can't make periodical commitments like this, then you may have to consider other types of investment that can grow without taking up your time.

Who to work with

Many investors make the mistake of thinking you can just walk into an estate agent, choose a house, buy it, have someone let it and watch the money roll in. You can't!

The first person you need to engage when thinking about property investment is an Independent Financial Adviser (IFA). Your mortgage will be the biggest cost involved in investing in buy-to-let and, for most people, it's the biggest debt they'll ever take on. So getting the right expert financial advice is vital.

An IFA should help you to:

- Identify your risk profile (how much risk versus reward you're prepared to take)
- Understand how property investment fits with your other income and investments
- Refine your investment objectives
- Understand how much money you can/should invest in buy-to-let
- Choose financial products that suit your particular circumstances and help you achieve your investment objectives.

Good financial planning is essential for profitable buy-to-let investing. And you MUST make sure the IFA you choose is truly independent, fully qualified to give advice on investments, understands the fundamentals of property investment and is regulated by the Financial Conduct Authority (FCA).

If you have a lot of different investments, and especially if your income puts you in a higher tax bracket, it may be a good move to engage someone who can advise you on the best way to structure your property investment business, in terms of tax, pension and inheritance planning.

Work with self-regulated letting agents who are members of a trade association to understand where the demand is in your investment area, and make sure you buy the right thing. Good agents will be happy to talk honestly with you – remember, these are the experts who are dealing with properties and tenants all day long, and they know what's in short supply, what rents well and which properties are likely to achieve the returns you're looking for.

...and who to avoid working with

Until your investment strategy and objectives have been established, you should avoid working with anyone except an IFA. After this has been done, you can carry out research into finance and specific properties types, tenant types and location.

Bear in mind that estate agencies – which is where many investors start – are staffed by salespeople. When they pitch a property to you, they're looking to get a sale *today* and they (typically) worry very little about you *tomorrow*. On top of that, there aren't many estate agents out there who *really* understand buy-to-let investing, so they're certainly not always the best people to be guiding you towards such a major investment.

Property Investment Clubs that pitch investments to you without knowing (or caring) about your particular objectives should be given a very wide berth. Companies offering 'armchair' investments – which we'll come on to in more detail later – should certainly be avoided at this stage.

· ·

Hot Tip

Whether you already have investment properties or are considering buying for the first time, take the time now to write down your investment objectives, what capital you can afford to have locked away for the next 15-20 years, and work out how much time you have spare to invest in buy-to-let. The results will determine what kind of property you should be investing in.

LandlordZONE® the UK's leading landlord website, providing property news, advice, legal information, comment and insight for the rental property industry since 1999

www.landlordzone.co.uk

CHAPTER 2
LANDLORD EDUCATION

The private rental sector is forever changing and you have to change, too. I have said many times before that you have to treat this as a business and with business comes a different set of rules. A landlord's biggest challenge now is to keep up with all this. You do not have to invest thousands of pounds into landlord education but you have to be pro-active.

My first port of call would be to join a landlord association, like the National Landlords Association (landlords.org.uk) or the Residential Landlords Association (rla.org.uk). For as little as £80 a year for membership, you will get access to all the latest news, legislation changes, advice on being compliant, information about campaigns, landlord views, guides, documentation, discounts to recommended suppliers, educational courses, local monthly meetings with other landlords, and a free telephone advice line.

At Landlord Action, a very common problem we have with landlords who instruct us is that they didn't know of a change in the law, or failed to serve relevant documentation. This is especially the case with those who have just one or two properties, and who still don't see themselves as landlords. Ignorance is not an excuse, and just costs landlords more money and time.

Attending property shows, such as The Property Investor Show and Landlord Investment Shows, can be useful, as they have suppliers exhibiting, seminars and debates, and provide networking opportunities with other landlords. They enable you to keep up to date with things and get a feel for the market.

The local authority responsible for the area where your properties are located may put on events for landlords, updating the council's position and sometimes providing guest speakers.

Look for networking groups in your area; Property Investors Network run more than 50 meetings a month nationwide for investors, landlords and suppliers to attend, and they are definitely worth a visit.

It's also worth signing up to webinars, when you can engage with a specialist in the property industry; I often do webinars for Rightmove, Upad, NALS, Urban and many others, as well as being booked to speak to landlords and letting agents at other events all over the country.

Go online and visit property portals regularly, making sure you sign up for updates and announcements. I can recommend website such as LandlordZONE, Property Tribes, Property 118, Landlord Today, Letting Agent Today, Property Reporter, Just Do Property and of course Propertychecklists.co.uk. Lastly, speak to other landlords, as you can learn a lot from them. Tap into their experience.

Remember: education is power.

CHAPTER 3
PREVENTING IDENTITY FRAUD

According to CIFAS, the UK's Fraud Prevention Service, identity fraud hit an all-time high in 2017, with 174,523 cases, up 1% from the previous year and a 125% increase on 10 years ago.
The Annual Fraud Indicator says identity theft cost £1.3bn in 2016.

As a property investor, you might think the only people you need to credit check are prospective tenants. Of course, they should be credit checked (and letting agents should undertake this for you) but they're not the only people being financially assessed – remember you're applying for a lot more credit than they are!

So it's essential you check your own credit rating before you make any financial applications, as it will affect how easily you can secure finance for your property investment.

A credit report gives a snapshot of all your credit accounts and financial history. This information is useful when you're evaluating financial products, such as mortgages, as it helps establish which products might be more appropriate for you.

A credit report will show all the applications for credit that have been made in your name, so checking your rating periodically means you should pick up any fraud.

A further key benefit of checking your credit rating is prevention of identity fraud. Remember, tenants could have access to your details from any post that arrives for you at a rented property, so make sure all your post is redirected away from the buy to let property in your name. If a crooked tenant has access to your personal details, they could carry out all different type of thefts and frauds, which could have a huge impact on your life.

I have heard some shocking stories of tenants taking over a landlord's identity, especially when the landlord is overseas and has no mortgage on the property. The criminal tenant has been able to fake the landlord's details and successfully remortgage in the landlord's name, getting the funds transferred to a fake bank account with the monies siphoned off. All without the landlord being aware.

The Land Registry has a fraud prevention service called Property Alert, which is worth a visit: https://propertyalert.landregistry.gov.uk/

Key steps

1. **Remove all personal documents from your rental property**
   Before you let a property, make sure you take away all documents relating to your personal or business affairs. And put them through a paper shredder, rather than just throwing them away.

2. **No personal post should be sent to the rental property**
   Make sure that all your post is redirected away from the buy to let property in your name. If a crooked tenant has access to your personal details, they could carry out all different type of thefts and frauds.

   If you're not sure whether there is any post in your name going to your rental property, consider setting up a three-month mail redirection via the Post Office. This will ensure all post comes to your current address and you can then amend it with services and suppliers as necessary.

3. **Register with the Mailing Preference Service**

   This helps to ensure your details are taken off most direct mail advertising databases and should prevent promotional mail that may contain sensitive information going to your rental properties. Register online at: mpsonline.org.uk

4. **Keep a note of whose name the utilities are in**

   After a tenant has left the property, some landlords change the utilities into their name. If you do this, remember to change them back to the new tenant's name from the day the tenancy starts.

5. **Check your statements and credit report**

   Although it can be a laborious task, all bills and statements should be checked as soon as possible. When a new credit card statement comes through, make sure it's accurate and correct. Ideally, check your bill alongside receipts for purchases you've made.

   If any entries or transactions seem suspect, contact the company or organisation straight away, otherwise you may not be covered for monies spent on your behalf and sorting out what you have paid for and what is fraud will be tricky.

   Check your credit score either monthly or at least once every six months.

If you think you've been a victim of identity fraud:

- Contact ALL your creditors, not just the ones you suspect are involved. This will alert companies that you may be a target and covers you, should further identity fraud take place.
- Contact a credit-referencing agency, such as Experian or Equifax, who can offer advice on what to do.
- Contact CIFAS, the UK's fraud prevention service. They can register you for Protective Registration – effectively, a note against your credit file

stating that you have been a victim of fraud and your identity is vulnerable, which helps prevent further fraud occurring. Visit: cifas.org.uk/pr

Who to work with

There are a number of services available for landlords to check their credit score. Equifax (www.equifax.co.uk) and Experian (www.experian.co.uk) are the most well-known providers and have instant access online services, where you can obtain your credit report initially for free and then for fees ranging from a few pounds to £15 per month.

Questions to ask

Once you've obtained a copy of your credit report, the key questions are:

Have there been any applications for credit in your name that you're unaware of?
If there are, you need to get in touch with the organisation that made the credit check to inform them that you may have been the victim of identity fraud. Individual processes of different companies will vary, but they all have an obligation to investigate further. Always follow up any phone calls in writing and, if necessary, send correspondence by recorded delivery so you have proof you identified a problem.

Are there any bad credit reports against your name?
It is possible for a company to put a bad credit report against your name without you knowing about it. Checking your credit record regularly will ensure you can take steps to remove any of these that you don't believe should be there.

Can you improve your credit rating?
Lenders and other organisations (credit cards, store accounts, etc) check your credit rating to see if you're a good person to lend money to. There are

ways of improving your credit rating, which will help make you a 'better bet' in the eyes of a lender and help you secure buy-to-let finance.

Contact any organisation that has noted bad credit marks against you and find out from them what steps you can take to restore a good credit status.

• •

Hot Tip

LAND REGISTRY: When registering your title for a property at the Land Registry, include a contact address that is NOT your rental property. You can register a restriction of your property title (by completing Land Registry Form RX1), which ensures that no transfer of registry can take place without the consent of the named party. Make sure you sign up to the free property alert service, which will inform you if anyone attempts to change the register: https://propertyalert.landregistry.gov.uk/

• •

Case Study

Laylah De Cruz and her mother Dianne Moorcroft were jailed for a £1.2m Kensington property fraud, after assuming the identity of a deceased landlord.

The Daily Mail reported that they conspired with others and managed to rent the property with fake references. When the tenancy was secured, Moorcroft changed her name by deed poll to that of the deceased landlord, opened bank accounts in Dubai with a UK passport, then secured a £1.2m loan against the property and spent the cash.

CHAPTER 4
FINANCING BUY-TO-LET PROPERTY

There were 5,100 buy-to-let mortgages in arrears by 2.5% or more of the outstanding balance in Q3 2017, according to UK Finance. In the same quarter, UK Finance reports that there were 600 buy-to-let repossessions.

Post-credit crunch, the mortgage market saw the number of buy-to-let mortgages available drastically reduce and then begin to increase again once the economy and property market started to recover.

Lenders are still more cautious about loaning money than they were prior to the credit crunch, so you'll have to work harder to ensure you can secure borrowing on the properties you want to buy or refinance.

Any deal you look at needs to be affordable in both the short and long term, so everybody taking out a mortgage – not just landlords – has to pass 'stress tests' to show they are able to meet the payments even if interest rates rise. And, as a landlord, your property management fees and tax liabilities, as well as your other sources of income, such as a salary, personal tax liabilities and living costs, will also be taken into account.

On top of this, you must make sure the yield will be great enough that your investment will remain cash positive into the future. Your lender may require the rental income to be up to 145% of the monthly mortgage payments. Requirements will vary from lender to lender, and are likely to be different for HMOs (Houses in Multiple Occupation).

You will also need deposit funds; so-called 'no money down' deals are – as things stand in 2018 – likely to be illegal. Expect to have to put down at least a 25% deposit on the majority of products with reasonable terms. You can get higher loan-to-value BTL mortgages, but bear in mind that interest rates will be higher on these products and it is more difficult to make them cashflow positive.

There are two main types of mortgage:
- Repayment – as well as interest, you pay off some of the capital each month;
- Interest-only – you only pay the interest and, at the end of the term, still owe the full amount borrowed.

From 30th September 2017, anyone with four or more mortgaged rental properties is considered to be a portfolio landlord and the whole portfolio will be considered when seeking finance for additional purchases. As a portfolio landlord, you will need to produce a business plan and provide potential lenders with evidence of income from all your properties and other sources, as well as your assets and liabilities.

Key steps

1. **Get your financial records in order**
   Take some time to gather together bank statements and proof of income, check your credit rating and make sure your deposit funds are in place and accessible in good time for exchange of contracts.

2. **Get the right specialist broker**
   Picking a buy-to-let mortgage is complex, so it's imperative you deal with experts in the field and, since the mortgage market is continuously evolving, it's important to find an adviser who is up to date with the latest buy-to-let products. Those who also have their own property portfolio are ideal, as they're more likely to appreciate your situation and be able to find the best products for your circumstances.

A good adviser/broker should easily be able to answer questions about the property market, how lenders view buy-to-let at the moment and talk through what future interest and mortgage rates might be over the next five to 10 years. If you're in any doubt, ask to speak to an investor who has been their client for five or more years.

3. **Be clear on what you're buying**
   Make sure you fully disclose to your broker how you intend to rent the property out, as that may make a difference to the available products, eg lending for HMOs can be quite limited.

4. **Double-check the deal**
   Regardless of how happy you are with your broker or adviser, it's a good idea to check the product they're suggesting with online comparison sites – it can help ensure you get the most competitive deal.

Who to work with

Specialist advice should be sought from mortgage brokers and independent financial advisers and it's vital you check these professionals have the right accreditations.

Any company that gives advice on mortgages *must* be regulated by the Financial Conduct Authority (FCA). Individuals who can advise on mortgage products will hold one or more of the following qualifications:

- **CertMA**: Certificate in Mortgage Advice
- **CeMAP**: Certificate in Mortgage Advice and Practice
- **MAPC**: Mortgage Advice and Practice Certificate (Scotland)

If someone does not have *at least one* of these qualifications, they are not legally able to advise you on mortgages.

Some advisers have access to mortgage offers that are unique to them, eg if they work in a bank, so it might be useful to contact several different advisers, rather than just one. And ask anyone who calls themselves 'independent' to confirm that they really are able to access all the products in the marketplace.

As lenders are not keen to lend to anyone that has little evidence of income – for example, if you're newly self-employed or have been a credit risk in the past – using a broker may help in finding the right mortgage deal.

A word of warning...
The FCA has noticed a misuse of buy-to-let and let-to-buy mortgages (for people who can't sell their existing home and therefore need to remortgage to finance the purchase of their new home) with some brokers recommending these mortgages to people who are simply struggling to secure finance. This could mean the customer is actually committing mortgage fraud, so make sure your mortgage adviser has a good track record over the last 5+ years of dealing with property investors.

Some key factors that affect buy-to-let lending:
- There are now three types of buy to let lending compliance and some lenders will only lend on certain types (some no longer let on consumer buy to let or portfolio landlords), although the tax and stamp duty rules are the same for all of them. They are:
  - Portfolio landlords – mainly professional landlords (but not always) who have more than four buy to let properties;
  - Consumer buy to let – when the property has been lived in by the landlord previously, or they have inherited it or have some other link to it
  - Business buy to let – when a landlord purchases a property he has never lived in and is solely buying for the purpose of letting out.
- Exposure – banks will not want an interest in more than a certain number of flats in a single development, or to have too many loans with one borrower.

- Development finance – banks are wary of allowing developers to use buy-to-let lending in place of commercial lending to either finance projects or 'cash-out' on project completion.
- Property type – flat above shops, ex-council, high rise with no lift, short lease length, etc… it may be hard to borrow against properties like these. Something worth noting about flats above shops is that businesses are not necessarily longer required to apply for permission for change of use, so the quiet shop below your flat could be turned into a restaurant, potentially disrupting your tenants' quality of life and making it harder to let in the future.
- Habitable property – buy-to-let lenders will not lend on property that is uninhabitable.
- Market rent – lending is based on the market rent of a property in its *current* condition, not the *potential* value (after refurbishment, etc)

Questions to ask

1. **Have you checked your credit score?**
   Chapter 3 explains the importance of knowing your credit score when applying for a mortgage and it's becoming more and more important. Just one late payment can wipe out 90% of available deals. It may be that you are able to improve your credit score, which could then increase the number of mortgages available to you.

   If you're considering a joint mortgage (eg if you're investing with a business partner or a spouse), it's important to check the credit score of both individuals. Also, ensure that there is a Deed of Trust in place.

2. **What type of mortgage can I get?**
   In order to get an answer to this, you'll need to answer some questions yourself regarding how you want to repay the loan, eg do you want to keep payments flexible and be able to take out capital when you want or do you want to fix your mortgage costs? Talk through your investment objectives with your mortgage adviser/broker.

3. **How much deposit do I need?**
   Ultimately, this depends on the types of mortgages you have access to, your credit rating and your investment objectives. If you have good credit, you'll probably find that you can get higher loan-to-value (LTV) mortgages. LTVs for buy-to-let mortgages are typically between 50% and 75%, so you need a deposit of between 25% and 50% of the property's value.

   The higher the deposit, the lower your monthly repayments will be, so you're likely to realise more rental profit. If, however, you're investing primarily for capital growth, a lower deposit may suit your investment objectives better.

4. **How much can I borrow?**
   Unlike lending against your primary residence, which is based on your earnings, buy-to-let mortgages are based primarily on the rental income potential, although most lenders will also want to see proof of earnings of at least £25,000 per annum.

   All lenders have a 'rental ratio' they will lend against, which typically ranges from 125% to 145% of the mortgage cost. (Most lenders currently base their cost calculation on a 'notional' interest rate that is higher than the actual rate, to reflect the possibility of interest rate rises in the future.) So, if you were looking to borrow an amount that would mean a monthly mortgage repayment of £1,000, you'd have to achieve rent of between £1,250 and £1,450 per month. You MUST make sure you use this calculation in working out your figures before you make an offer on a property – you don't want to get to the mortgage valuation stage and suddenly find out things don't stack up.

   If your purchase will result in you owning four or more mortgaged rental properties, you will become a portfolio landlord, and be subject to further affordability checks, which will include looking at your whole portfolio, income, assets and liabilities, and past and future cash flow.

5. What fees are applicable?

Up-front fees for arranging your mortgage represent a big cost that you have to pay out when investing in buy-to-let. Fees vary by lender and are lower the more competitive the marketplace is.

Request a schedule of all fees from the lender prior to applying for a mortgage. You don't just pay fees for organising the mortgage; lenders may charge fees when you sell the property, take out a further loan, redeem the mortgage early or if you make late payments.

6. Do I need an independent survey?

Getting an independent survey from a member of the Royal Institution of Chartered Surveyors (RICS) is essential. People often confuse a survey with a mortgage valuation, which is carried out to protect the lender, not you. A Condition Report will give you a view on any necessary repairs, while a HomeBuyer or Building survey will give you an independent view on the property's current value and highlight any issues you need to take care of now and in the future, to ensure the property is in good condition.

••

Hot Tip

DON'T OVERSTRETCH YOURSELF: Part of the cause of the credit crunch was people taking out loans on which they couldn't afford to make the repayments. This inevitably led to them defaulting and, in many cases, having their properties repossessed. The aim of investment is to increase wealth, not decrease it, so make sure you can afford to operate your buy-to-let portfolio whatever the circumstances.

CHAPTER 5
WHO IS YOUR BUY TO LET FOR?

Before you invest in a property, it's important to understand what types of tenants will enable the let to deliver on your investment objectives.

Different types of tenants will have different requirements and deliver different returns, so you need to match the two and ensure the property you buy and rent meets both your and their expectations.

Key steps

1. Make sure you understand yield
Yield is a common term used in buy-to-let to compare the return you receive versus the value of the property and is a good way of generally measuring one type and location of investment against another one.

Gross yield is generally calculated by dividing the rent by the value of the property. For example:

Property purchase price: £200,000
Annual rent: £15,000
£15,000 (rent) divided by £200,000 (price) = 0.075
Multiply 0.075 by 100 to get the yield as a percentage

Therefore, the yield is 7.5%.

The problem with this simple calculation is it doesn't take into account all the costs involved. The real test is to measure the net yield by including the annual running costs (fees, refurbishment, maintenance, management costs, etc). Assuming they came to £5,000, that brings the net rental income down to £10,000 and the net yield down to 5%. If you are considering buying through a property investment club or sourcer, then make sure you're clear about exactly how they've calculated the potential yield they're quoting.

Typically, higher yields come from higher-risk tenant types, such as individuals renting rooms. Lower-risk tenant types, such as families or professional couples, will generally result in lower yields.

2. Look at the different types of tenants and the risk versus reward of each

Professionals: Someone employed who earns above average income and looks to rent for six months plus. They typically want a property of a fairly high standard that they can move straight into, in a nice area within easy reach of work and a town/city centre.

Risk profile: Professional tenants rarely fall into rent arrears, but if they do, it is important to act quickly. You should also be aware that there are 'professional bad tenants', who look and act very respectable, but who make a habit of defaulting on rent and know the eviction laws better than most landlords. Always ask for bank statements and a previous landlord's reference as part of your referencing process.

Corporate short-term lets: Specialist types of let, which require a high-spec property with modern amenities and including bed linen and cutlery.

Risk profile: This is probably the least risky tenant type, as all the rent is usually paid up front and all bills are included, however if you have a mortgage, you need to check the lender will allow this type of agreement.

Tenants of Homes in Multiple Occupation: An HMO is broadly defined as a property where there are three or more unrelated people, who have their own bedroom but share kitchen and bathroom facilities. The property could be a flat or a house. Visit https://www.gov.uk/house-in-multiple-occupation-licence for the full definition.

However, local authorities now have the power to decide on their own definition of HMOs and licensing, which means that some areas require all HMOs to be licensed, while others stick to the standard licensing definition of five or more people sharing a property that is over three or more floors. In October 2018, this standard definition changed so the number of storeys is no longer relevant. Always check local licensing rules and regulations.

In some areas you will also need to seek planning permission. Contact your local authority at an early stage to make sure you abide by their rules and regulations and join a local accredited landlord scheme (if there is one) to make sure you receive notification of any changes in legislation.

In addition to licensing, HMOs may require certain fixtures and fittings, eg fire doors, extinguishers and alarms, and have to abide by a number of specific health and safety rules and regulations.

Risk profile: People who want to rent a room often include students, people on low incomes, migrant workers and part-time workers, all of whom may not be there for very long, meaning frequent check-ins and check-outs. Their employment can have very little security, they tend to be younger and they often don't take particular care of the property. And if you don't abide by all the local HMO rules and regulations, you can face fines, which could run into tens of thousands of pounds.

Social tenants. This is where your tenant is receiving some form of benefit from the state to help pay their rent. It doesn't necessarily mean they aren't working, it just means they're getting some payment from the state. If you're considering letting to social tenants, contact the local authority housing department and they will advise you what kind of properties are in short supply and what a tenant could afford to pay. Be aware that you can't always rent to tenants in receipt of Local Housing Allowance (LHA) or Universal Credit (UC), as your lender and/or insurer may restrict the type of tenants you have.

Risk profile: Social tenants can be great, as they tend to be less mobile than professionals or students, so stay in your property for longer, and you experience fewer voids because of the huge demand for social housing. The main issue is that your rent is likely to be reliant on what happens to the tenant's income, as Local Housing Allowance is replaced by Universal Credit. This affects how their money is paid to them and, in turn, to you. Typically, LHA is paid to the tenant, who is responsible for passing this money on to you and, if they don't, getting your rent paid tends to depend on how helpful the local housing office is. With Universal Credit, this help is likely to disappear, although landlords can apply for an Alternative Payment Arrangement (APA) Managed Payment to Landlord (MPTL) which will be considered on a case by case basis. However, this is likely to be time-consuming and can mean you wait months for payment, or your claim may be rejected.

You can work with your tenant to have them classed as 'vulnerable', which might help ensure the rent is paid directly to you. Another way to reduce your risk is to include all bills in the rent, as they are less likely to default on electricity or other utility payments.

The other major risk consideration is the government's moves to reduce the amount of benefit money social tenants receive. That would mean the rent you could charge a social tenant could be significantly less than for a professional, particularly in London and the South East. Current levels of housing benefit available to tenants can be seen at: voa.gov.uk/corporate/RentOfficers/LHADirect.html

3. Refurbish/furnish your property appropriately

Each tenant profile will have different requirements. The best people to speak to in order to make sure you get this right are local letting agents, who know what tenants are really looking for. Corporate lets will require a higher standard of fixtures, fittings and furnishings and therefore a greater investment on your part. Students and LHA will only need a simple, hardwearing finish and that should be a lower investment for you although, from October 2018, there are minimum room sizes for HMOs. Make sure you're clear on what your target market needs and wants and factor the related costs into your purchase budget.

Where is your buy to let?

In the UK, Wales, Scotland, Northern Ireland and England all have separate housing policies – and their own laws. Much of this book will be relevant for every region, but it is important to be aware of the differences.

Scotland

There have been significant changes to the Scottish rental market in recent times, which are markedly different from the rest of the United Kingdom.

From 1st December 2017, landlords cannot offer Short Assured Tenancies and new tenants effectively have indefinite tenure.

On 1 December, Scottish landlords were no longer able to sign a new Short Assured Tenancy. Instead, they have to sign a new type of agreement called a Private Residential Tenancy, which gives tenants greater security. No-fault evictions and fixed terms are no longer allowed, although there are now 18 grounds for eviction; a mix of mandatory and discretionary.

Notice periods must be at least 84 days if the tenant has occupied the property for more than six months (28 days if the tenant has lived there for less than this). Tenants don't have to serve the full 84 days' notice; they can submit reciprocal notice, which is 28 days, regardless of the length of occupancy.

Only one rent increase will be allowed per year, with three months' notice, and disputed increases can be referred to a rent officer.

Landlords must register with the Landlord Registration central online system for Scotland and also notify the local authority if they appoint a letting agent. Since 31st January 2018, anyone carrying out residential letting agent work

– ie letting on behalf of another – has been bound by a Letting Agent Code of Practice and, from 1st October 2018, they will have to be registered.

HMO landlords – letting to three or more unrelated people sharing facilities such as kitchen or bathroom – must have a licence.

There are strict rules and regulations on the condition a property has to be in to be let out, including ensuring the property's electrical installation meets the Repairing Standard and the property itself meets a level of repair known as the Tolerable Standard. In addition, mains-powered and interlinked smoke alarms, a heat alarm and fire extinguishers must be installed.

Any necessary legal action will be taken against the landlord, even those who use a letting agent.

For more information on Scotland, visit:
scotland.gov.uk/Topics/Built-Environment/Housing/privaterent
rentingscotland.org/

Wales
Wales passed a new housing bill in 2014 that made major changes to the private rented sector.

All landlords who rent in Wales on an assured, assured shorthold or regulated tenancy must register with Rent Smart Wales. In addition, landlords must either use a trained and licensed agent or, if self-managing, undertake training and apply for their own licence, which should be renewed every five years.

For more information, visit: www.rentsmart.gov.wales/en/

Northern Ireland
All landlords in Northern Ireland have to be registered.
For more information visit:
www.nidirect.gov.uk/articles/landlord-registration-scheme

HMO landlords must also register with the Housing Executive.

Who to work with

Recommended letting agents that belong to a self-regulated trade organisation and your local council – especially if you're operating an HMO or dealing with tenants receiving Local Housing Allowance or Universal Credit.

Questions to ask

Am I happy with the projected yield? Can I definitely charge the rent I need to achieve the profit I need/want?

··

Hot Tip

IDENTIFY TARGET TENANTS: Not all properties are suitable for all tenant types, so make sure you're clear on who you want to rent to before you buy a property.

CHAPTER 6
BUYING THROUGH AN ESTATE AGENT

Estate agents that understand how property investment works can be extremely useful to you as a buy-to-let investor. But do remember they're paid to act on the vendor's behalf and it's illegal for them to do any deals with you that would be deemed not in the seller's interest. As all estate agents now have to belong to a redress scheme, they have come under much more scrutiny and need to ensure they abide by strict codes of practice.

Do be very wary of property investment 'training companies' that run 'How to work with an estate agent' courses, which tend to teach you how to get properties cheaply – and charge you for the privilege! In my opinion, that's a totally unnecessary expense. And the truth is, if you do find an agent that deliberately sells you properties at less than they *could* sell them for, they are likely to be acting illegally and could be implicating you in the process. For example, any repossession instructions they receive have to have to be promoted via the local press and portals to ensure there are no other potential bidders out there – there's no shortcut to getting 'exclusivity' on these kinds of deals.

Key steps

1. **Try to find estate agents who understand buy-to-let**
   Ideally, you want to work with agents who understand the difference between which properties and roads are the most popular and which properties can offer similar rents but cost less to purchase. That will enhance your yield and profit, essentially making a better investment.

   Some agents will just want to sell you any property they have on their books and get the highest price for their client. Others will see you as someone who simply wants a cheap bargain and will therefore get in the way of them achieving a good sale price for their vendor. You need to work out which agents are going to be able to work effectively with you.

Good agents will spend time talking to you and understanding your investment objectives. Many of them will also be able to secure deals on properties from part-exchange companies and from lenders or developers who are motivated to sell quickly and are able to reduce the price accordingly.

2. Present yourself as a serious professional investor

Really, all you need to do to get the best out of an agent is build a good relationship with them. To become someone they'll contact with the best deals, make sure you prove to them:

- You have funds available
- You will view a property within 24 hours and usually the same day that they call you
- You can decide quickly whether to make an offer and will complete on the deal
- You have already lined up a good legal company, surveyor and mortgage adviser, all of whom can work to tight deadlines to purchase a property in a matter of weeks.

3. Additional services you may be offered

Most estate agents will recommend their contacts, eg a mortgage broker or solicitor, and will often try to insist on you speaking to their broker so they can confirm you have the appropriate finance in place before putting forward any offer. Don't presume they're prying or trying to force you to use their services; it's usually just part of their due diligence process. Just make sure you have your own contacts' details to hand to put their minds at rest. Agents are not allowed to hold back properties or viewings from anyone who has declined their third-party services, so don't allow yourself to be bullied into taking advice.

These recommended services might be worth investigating but pursue your own independent contacts, too. One reason is that firms recommended as standard may not be able to guarantee you the speed and quality of service you want and need.

Secondly, not all will be buy-to-let specialists. And, thirdly, the legal and financial advice you receive really MUST go hand in hand – and take into account all your financial interests, not just property – so you need to be confident you have considered and independently chosen the best people for *you*.

Who to work with

Estate/letting agents
When buying and letting, only use agents which are operating legally in the UK and are members of an ombudsman.

Estate agents and letting agents should belong to a trade association which has its own codes of conduct and high ethical standards that must be adhered to. They should also hold relevant qualifications from the relevant organisation.

Partly the reason for securing an agent that is already qualified is because of three major changes which will take place over the next year or so:

1. Client Money Protection
Make sure your agent has Client Money Protection as this will become a legal requirement from 1st April 2019. Those agents who don't already have CMP may find they cannot secure it, so will then be operating illegally and may be forced to close. ARLA and RICS agents already have to have CMP to be members. Go to www.clientmoneyprotect.co.uk for more information.

2. Letting fees ban

Agents are soon to lose revenue from the loss of letting fees which may render some agents unprofitable and force them to close.

3. Agent regulation

In addition, letting agents and property managers will need to be regulated in the future, which means self-regulated agents are the best ones to choose now as they are the ones who are most likely to survive these substantial changes.

Be suspicious of an agent who asks you to transfer money through them. Any money exchanged during the purchase/sale of property must go through a legal company. Never accept bank sort codes or account numbers via email due to scams. Always call the legal company to confirm where to send the money.

Be aware of additional regulations which apply in Scotland and Wales, and ensure your agent complies. For instance, since 31st January 2018, letting agents in Scotland have been bound by a Letting Agent Code of Practice and will have to be registered from midnight on 1st October 2018.

Solicitors/conveyancers

Never use a 'cheap' conveyancer! Buy-to-let investing means you incur taxes both when you take income and when you sell the property. To keep the taxes as low as possible, you need to be sure you are purchasing property in the correct legal way for your circumstances – and that takes specialist advice.

Make sure they are currently accredited by the Law Society or Council of Licensed Conveyancers to protect you, should anything go wrong.

Remember: as a consumer, you have a choice of who to use as a service provider. You are not obliged to use a legal company that has been recommended by the agent.

Mortgage brokers/advisers

Securing the right buy-to-let mortgage is vital, as it can make or break your investment. You're likely to need a very specific mortgage for your investment strategy, so go back and re-read Chapter 4!

Remember:

- Agents can earn a commission for referring business to a mortgage broker
- No-one can legally give you financial advice without currently being registered with the Financial Conduct Authority
- Different mortgage advisers may give you different recommendations, so take two or three comparisons and work out how much you will pay each of them for their services.
- If you have four or more properties, you are considered a portfolio landlord and will require a business plan

Questions to ask

If you have built a good rapport with an agent, this will make it easier to ask lots more questions about the property and the vendor to ensure you purchase at a price that works for you.

1. **How long has the property been on the market?**
   The longer it has, the more likely the vendor is to consider a lower offer.

2. **Is the vendor under pressure to sell quickly?**
   If time pressure is greater than money pressure, it's easier to negotiate a discount.

3. **What is the real reason for the sale?**
   As with points 1 and 2, this will give you an idea of whether you're going to be able to make a deal at a discount from the asking price, eg is it a distressed sale (ie has to be sold due to impending

repossession) or is the seller in a chain and committed to buying another property?

4. Is the property in probate?

If so, you need to find out where it is in the legal process: has probate been granted and how many executors or beneficiaries are you dealing with. The process could take a long time and there may be complications.

5. What is the property's EPC rating?

From 1st April 2018, only properties with an EPC rating of E and above can be legally let (although some exemptions apply). If the property's EPC rating is F or G, find out what work will be required to bring it up to standard, and how much this will cost, as this could both eat into your budget and mean you are unable to let immediately.

....

Hot Tip

TRUST YOUR INSTINCTS: If an agent doesn't understand your needs or doesn't see the benefit of working with an investor, don't deal with them.

....

Case Study

An estate agent in Berkhamsted was jailed for 18 months for fraud. The Hertfordshire Mercury reported that James Beck took out loans totalling £30k in the name of a woman whose house he was selling. He opened up an account in her name, took out two £15k loans in 2016 and used some of the money to go on holiday to Mexico.

The judge said: "You are a deeply devious and dishonest human being."

In this case, the agents would have had the personal information of their client and this rogue employee abused his position.

CHAPTER 7
BUYING THROUGH AN INVESTMENT CLUB

I estimate, from all the complaints we have received against property investment clubs, that over a million pounds of investors' hard-earned cash has been taken without a single property being delivered.

Although our business is primarily handling landlord possession actions, over the last 18 years I've increasingly been contacted by people with complaints against property investment clubs. To date, hundreds of people have reported property clubs that have taken their money and either not delivered any property or – often worse – delivered property that has then lost them substantial amounts in terms of equity and/or rent.

Property investment companies tend to work in two ways. They will either source properties for you, for a 'finder's fee', or they offer you an 'armchair' service, where you pay them usually tens of thousands of pounds to buy, let and manage properties for you.

In both cases, you're essentially trusting in someone else's skill and ability to find property that will make a good investment for you. Some property investment clubs are worth working with, as they provide a good service and can help ensure you don't make mistakes that could cost you now and in the future, but there are still far too many cowboys out there.

There is currently no legislation requiring property investment clubs to be regulated, so you need to make sure you're asking the right questions to be able to sort the good from the bad.

Doing due diligence on the property investing company is absolutely imperative. This includes:

- looking up their company accounts online
- making sure they don't have any County Court Judgements
- going onto property forums such as Propertytribes.com to seek feedback from other investors

Rent to Rent

I am seeing more and more people getting into the Rent to Rent industry to increase cashflow, especially at property networking events.

Rent to Rent sees letting agents and property managers offer landlords guaranteed rent on longer-term contracts. When signing a Rent to Rent agreement, the landlord is giving the renter consent to sublet the property. These contracts should never be Assured Shorthold Tenancies but should be commercial lease agreements.

Landlords seeking guaranteed rent agreements generally do so for peace of mind. They like to know their property will be rented for longer and their rent will be paid. Even though they generally receive below market rent, it means they prevent void periods, and reletting and letting agent fees. On top of this, maintenance is taken care of for them.

If using a rent guarantee company, do seek legal advice, as it's important to ensure you are signing a correct legal contract. There are good companies, such as Northwood, who offer a great service.

When it works, it works well. Every landlord wants peace of mind.
But when it goes wrong, it can go terribly wrong.

An agent or a renter could:

1. Fail to forward on the rent
2. Fail to maintain the property

3. Put the landlord at risk of prosecution from the local council by overcrowding the property and not complying with HMO regulations and licensing

Ultimately, as a landlord, you can lose control of the property you own because the occupier (sub-tenant) is not your tenant. This can, for example, make possession proceedings complicated because your claim is against the guaranteed rent company rather than the occupant.

Over the last few years, I have seen the Rent to Rent/guaranteed rent industry increase massively, due to the shared economy and the strain on the housing market. Some tenants – especially in places like London where rents are so high – can't afford to rent single units such as studio and one-bed flats, so opt for room lets in shared accommodation

Because of this increase we are constantly working on evictions on Rent to Rent/subletting cases.

In my view, problems arise if the agreement and process are not carried out diligently. Any agent offering guaranteed rent, or Rent to Rent, must:

1. be compliant
2. understand the rules and regulations in renting out property
3. belong to a redress scheme such as the Property Redress Scheme, by law, as they are accepting rent and deposits. If they fail to belong to a redress scheme, they could be fined up to £5,000 by Trading Standards.
4. have Professional Indemnity Insurance and Client Money Protection

So make sure you check before committing yourself.

Unfortunately, if you become involved in a suspect or even illegal Rent to Rent scheme or property investment club, by the time you realise there is a problem, the club has moved on to the 'next big money maker', leaving you to pick up the pieces.

But there are some good companies, such as Northwood, Orchard & Shipman, and Caridon Property, who offer a tried and tested guaranteed rent service to landlords, paying the rent every month and covering any void periods.

I wrote some guides on Rent to Rent for the Property Redress Scheme website (www.theprs.co.uk); they are a useful resource for landlords, agents and tenants involved in guaranteed rent schemes.

A word of warning…

Just because the guaranteed rent company is not renting directly to the occupant, it is not exempt from the usual landlord rules and regulations.

Key steps

Before you sign up to any kind of agreement with a guaranteed rent scheme or investment club, make sure you carry out the following due diligence:

1. Google the company and individuals involved and check their credentials with Landlord Action and Propertychecklists.co.uk
2. Run an individual check on the directors of the company to ensure they haven't been bankrupt in the past
3. Check out the contract with Landlord Action or another legal company
4. Make sure the company confirms in writing that any money you give them will be held in a separate 'client account'
5. Ask for references from other clients and go and visit some of their properties
6. Ask for a clear explanation of how the returns being quoted have been calculated

7. Make sure they're happy for you to have any deal independently valued and/or appraised
8. Do a County Court Judgment search on the company, to see if anything untoward shows up
9. Does this company have lots of sister companies? Make sure you research all that are in the same 'group'.

Who to work with

Although there's currently no blanket legal requirement for regulation, any company you use to help you secure investment deals should ideally be regulated by a third party at some level. For example, ideally they should have signed up to a redress scheme such as The Property Redress Scheme or The Property Ombudsman. If the company offers finance as well as properties, they should be registered with the Financial Conduct Authority.

Questions to ask

There are some key questions to ask property investment clubs so you can work out who is worth talking to – and who to avoid!

1. Do they require fees up front? If they do, don't give them a penny!
2. Do they insist on you using their mortgage or legal company? If so, run away!
3. Are they offering 'no money down deals' or 'properties for £1'? If so, they're likely to be acting illegally or recommending very high risk, untested investments.
4. Are they happy for you to visit the property before purchase and send in your own RICS surveyor? If not, there's something suspicious going on.
5. Can they clearly explain and substantiate the discounts and gains they're quoting, and if they're saying returns are 'guaranteed', are they prepared to put that in writing? When returns sound too good to be true, they usually are.

6. Are the directors and senior people within the company buying into these kinds of properties themselves? If not, ask them why not!

If you do get involved with an investment club and they don't deliver, it will be very difficult to get your money back, so make sure you do your own due diligence first.

....

Hot Tip

SMALL CLAIMS COURT: If you have a dispute over money with a company and the amount is under £10,000, it only costs around £100 to take them to the Small Claims Court. Trying to get your money back via the main courts could cost tens of thousands of pounds.

....

Case Study

Beware of self-professed 'property gurus'. Phil Martin was a high profile property guru, speaking at all the network meetings on the wealth education circuit, where he sold people expensive mentoring programmes and a portfolio-building service, selling properties and specialising in lease options. But his Rapid Group ran into financial trouble, he was made bankrupt in 2009 and it is believed he owed investors in the region of £2.4 million.

As reported on Propertytribes.com he was convicted of six counts of fraud, imprisoned for 20 months and banned from being a company director for seven and a half years.

CHAPTER 8
MAKING SURE YOU LEGALLY OWN YOUR INVESTMENT IN THE RIGHT WAY

As I've said already, buy-to-let is a niche area of the property field and you need to work with specialists who understand buying and letting property as a business. Investing in tailored legal advice will help ensure your ownership is set up in the right way from a tax perspective.

When you're buying a property to let, there is more for the legal company to do than when someone is just buying their own home. For example, they need to check whether you're allowed to rent the property out – especially if you're buying a flat – and whether there is anything specific in the property's covenant that may stop you from renting the property to certain tenants.

The potential for crime...
Most legal companies, by their very nature, abide by the law. But as the money changing hands in property transactions typically goes through the legal company's accounts and can easily run into millions of pounds, it's clearly a great temptation for some individuals and even criminal gangs.

Since the credit crunch, we have seen a number of legal companies and solicitors moving around from firm to firm, committing fraud.

And this situation could get worse in the future. For the first time, companies can offer legal services even if the owners of the company are not solicitors. This means that any company can employ solicitors and conveyancers to carry out legal work. With more companies competing for your legal business, there is a greater possibility they won't necessarily be as robust as others have been in the past.

As in all areas of property investment, there are good and bad, and finding the right legal services provider boils down to your due diligence.

Who to work with

First, the legal company you work with must be a current member of the Law Society or Council for Licensed Conveyancers.

Then you need to make sure they understand:

1. Your investment objectives
2. The importance of tax implications and how to mitigate them
3. Legal clauses in the property deeds and contract that may conflict with your objectives
4. How to work with other experts, such as a mortgage broker, tax specialist and independent financial adviser or wealth manager
5. The importance of preparing a will that meets all your inheritance wishes and, if required, sets up trusts and insurance products to mitigate tax.

Don't forget to ask for a complete breakdown of their quote. Ideally, they should work on a 'no purchase, no fee' and fixed-fee basis.

Poor and unscrupulous companies will:

1. Try to charge you an hourly rate for conveyancing work, without any estimates of what the final bill will be
2. Claim they charge a low fee, then miss off their quote lots of additional charges you have to pay (stamp duty, disbursements, money transfer fees, etc.)
3. Take on too many cases per employee so they don't proactively chase your purchase or sale.
4. Not have any understanding of the buy-to-let process, including renting legals, tax, trusts and wills.

Questions to ask

Specific questions to ask any legal company you're considering:

1. How many property investors do they currently act for?
2. How long have they been acting on behalf of property investors?
3. Do they understand the implications of buying a property for your specific tenant type, eg a licensed House in Multiple Occupation?
4. Will they work with your tax and financial adviser or do they have contacts they work with that they would recommend to you?

•••

Hot Tip

TENANTS IN COMMON: Most buy-to-let investors who buy with a spouse or business partner should buy properties under 'tenants in common' not 'joint tenancy'. Check with your legal company and tax expert how you currently own your properties or intend to buy them, to ensure that you own properties in the right legal way for your particular situation.

CHAPTER 9
PREPARING YOUR PROPERTY FOR LET

When preparing a property for let, there are two main things you need to take into account. First, you must make sure you comply with anything required by law to let the property and, secondly, you must prepare and present the property in a way that appeals to your target tenant type.

Letting a property legally
Some legislation governing buy-to-let is national, some individual to a country within the UK – ie England or Scotland – and some is regional, typically local authority based. For example, licensed Houses in Multiple Occupation (HMOs) have national guidelines, but their definition and safety requirements are set by your local housing authority, which is given the freedom to interpret and add to the national guidelines.

Housing Standards and Fire Safety are two areas that you really do need to make sure you get right. Planning and building regulations issues can prove inconvenient and may cost you money to put right retrospectively, but if something goes wrong with the electrics or gas that subsequently causes harm to a tenant, you could be sent to jail.

If you employ a letting agent, some responsibility will be passed to them, but you still have to correctly implement everything you are advised to do.

Letting a property to your tenant type
In my experience, many of the disputes between landlords and tenants arise because the standard of the property has fallen below the tenants' expectations. You shouldn't be spending a fortune, but it is vital to maintain a property to a high standard. It should be clean and easy to keep that way; in good condition, with no mould, damp or cracks; showers, boilers, radiators, windows and doors should be in good working order.

The property must be maintained to this standard throughout the tenancy.

Key steps

1. **Consult your local council.**
   You will need to consult with several different departments to ensure you comply with all legislation, including Planning, Building Control, Private Sector Housing Health & Safety and Fire Safety. Different departments rarely seem to communicate with each other, so it's your responsibility to make sure you've spoken to everyone you need to.

2. **Does the property need planning permission or to be licensed?**
   If you're letting a property to multiple tenants, make sure you're very clear on the planning and licensing regulations for your area, as it can vary wildly. Some regions require planning permission for change of use if three or more unrelated people are sharing a house; others will allow six. Licensing broadly only applies if there are five or more unrelated tenants, but you do need to check this definition with the council. The definition of a licensed HMO changed October 2018; currently only properties of three or more storeys are considered HMOs, but the number of floors no longer forms part of the criteria.

3. **Are you affected by Building Regulations?**
   This concerns the health and safety of your tenants and covers a number of areas, including sound insulation, electrical and gas systems, and materials and insulation used for any renovation/ refurbishment. A surveyor will be able to advise you on this, but you MUST investigate BEFORE you start any work.

4. **Other health and safety requirements.**
   Do check these for your individual country and local authority to keep up to date with changes

Gas and electricity:

- All gas appliances must be checked by a Gas Safe registered person, ideally before and after the let.
- Gas certificates must be stored safely and renewed annually.
- Carbon monoxide detectors should be installed – this is a legal requirement where there is a solid fuel appliance but strongly advised wherever there is a gas appliance, too.
- All wiring and electrical modifications need to be carried out by a Part P qualified electrician and checked as often as the qualified electrician recommends. The government has announced that five-year electrical installation checks will become mandatory, although a date has not been announced.
- Heating systems must be adequate.

(See Chapter 10 for more detailed information.)

Fire regulations:

If available, arrange for a fire safety check, your local housing officer or fire service may be able to advise you, otherwise visit www.gov.uk/government/publications/fire-safety-in-shared-or-rented-accommodation for other advice on best practice for ensuring your tenants' safety. General steps you should take are:

- Installation of smoke alarms – it is a legal requirement for landlords to provide one on each floor of a rental property, and ideally these should be mains-powered, not battery. They should be tested on the first day of the tenancy, after which is the tenant's responsibility to test them regularly.
- Heat sensors and carbon monoxide detectors are also recommended, and legal requirements in some cases – again, these should ideally be powered by mains and tested regularly.

- Ensure there is a means of escape in the event of a fire, without having to cross an area containing electrical equipment.
- Have a fire extinguisher and fire blanket in the kitchen.

In HMOs, also:

- Fit fire doors
- Put up fire exit signs
- Ensure the fire alarm system is hard-wired and has a main control panel.

5. Certification

You must make sure that your administration of the necessary certificates is up to date. If you have a letting agent who manages the property, they will take care of most of this for you, but be aware that checks need to be carried out periodically, so set up some sort of diary reminder of when tests and checks are due or work with an agent that will do this for you.

- Gas safety certificate for all appliances (annual inspection)
- Safety checks for all electric installations (annual or as recommended)
- Portable Appliance Testing for any electrical appliances more than a year old (annual)
- Energy Performance Certificate (every 10 years)
- Confirmation that all products and furnishings comply with fire safety standards (on-going)

(See Chapter 10 for more detailed information.)

6. Instruction manuals

Keep a file in the property with manuals and operating instructions for all appliances.

7. Put together a team of contractors you can trust

If you're using a letting agent, they will have their own team, but you may not use them forever and having a good team of people you can call on for maintenance issues is incredibly important. I'd suggest you have in your contacts, as a minimum:

- General handyman
- Plumber
- Electrician
- Cleaner

Reliable contractors you can call on quickly and trust to do a good job are worth their weight in gold!

Who to work with

To ensure your property is legally let and kept in good condition, you will need to call on a whole host of services and contacts. Companies required to ensure your property is legally let include:

- Gas Safe Registered Engineer: www.gassaferegister.co.uk
- Part P Electrician: www.napit.org.uk, www.niceic.com, www.eca.co.uk
- Plumber: watersafe.org.uk
- PAT tester: pat-testing.info
- Fenestration Self-Assessment Scheme (double glazing): www.fensa. co.uk

If you're letting the property through a letting agent, make sure they belong to a trade association so you can be confident they know all the latest legal requirements and have a redress scheme, should anything go wrong.

Generally speaking, tradesmen and contractors are best found by local recommendation, but do be careful – there are far too many 'rogue' workmen who offer to work for cash. That means the cost of the work is not tax deductible for you and it's very difficult to pursue them if something goes wrong.

Five clear steps to avoiding bad workmen:

1. Don't use them if they don't currently work on buy-to-let properties and don't understand your responsibilities as a landlord.
2. Ensure you check any membership of a professional body. Some claim to be members and even have false identification, so go online and check they really are registered with a scheme – a good website to use is Checkatrade.com or the scheme's website itself.
3. Don't do deals for cash – you need official invoices to claim costs against tax.
4. For larger jobs, have a contract and get it checked by your solicitor.
5. Don't pay up front for large works. Agree stage payments and hold back 10% of the costs until a month after the job is finished, to allow for snagging issues to come to light. But don't hold back any other payment unless there is a real reason to dispute their workmanship.

Visit Propertychecklists.co.uk for more help finding quality tradesmen.

Questions to ask

It's vital you employ people who are reputable and keep up with the latest industry regulations, but you must also make sure you work with people who understand your responsibility as a landlord and appreciate that tenants typically want to be looked after straight away and not wait a week for things to be fixed!

So make sure you ask the following questions of anyone you're considering employing:

1. What experience do they have of working with buy-to-let investors and tenants?
2. Do they know the latest regulations landlords need to abide by?
3. What's their typical lead time, from call to visiting the property and fixing the problem?
4. What emergency services can they offer if required?
5. Do they charge by the hour or do they have fixed fees?

· ·

Hot Tip

GET A CARBON MONOXIDE DETECTOR: According to the Office of National Statistics, in England and Wales there are around 50 deaths between 2015 and 2016 from accidental carbon monoxide poisoning. In 2011 the government estimated that more than 4,000 people attend hospital emergency departments with low-level carbon monoxide poisoning per year and 200 are admitted.

A CO detector is compulsory in rental properties with a solid fuel appliance but strongly recommended in all properties with a gas appliance. For the sake of just £15-£20, install one as standard and make sure your property is safe for tenants.

CHAPTER 10
ENSURING YOUR APPLIANCES AND UTILITIES ARE SAFE FOR THE TENANT

It's incredibly important you make sure all the appliances you supply in a property that are powered by, or have access to gas, electricity or water, are safe. You have a duty of care to your tenants and it's vital that you can prove at any time that:

a.   you have done everything you can to provide a safe property, and
b.   you have responded to and resolved any issues that the tenant reports as quickly as possible.

To do this, you need to keep a copy of all your records and note down any contact you have from the tenant – even if it's just a text or phone call.

You will need to keep:

1.   All safety certificates
2.   A record of dates when safety certificates need to be reviewed
3.   Invoices from electricians, gas safety engineers and other workmen.
4.   Records of any checks you carried out on workmen to ensure they were properly qualified.
5.   A list, by tenant, of any conversations or contact with tenants over utility or appliance issues. You need to record the date, time and type of communication; what you did to fix the problem and when, and what the outcome was. Summarise the issues raised and send the tenant(s) a letter to confirm resolution.

If an appliance is unsafe it can cause injury to your tenant and, in the worst case, death. As a landlord, you are liable for the repercussions if you can be shown to have been negligent.

There are five areas you need to pay particular attention to:

- Gas and electrical safety
- Fire safety
- Condensation and heating
- Water
- Energy efficiency

Key steps

1. **Read the Health and Safety Executive's guidelines**
   This outlines the regulations that landlords must comply with. They also have a free advice line for landlords to clarify anything that they are unsure of – details of this and a copy of the guidelines are available on their website: hse.gov.uk

2. **Gas safety**
   Any individual who performs work on gas installations or appliances within a property must be registered with the Gas Safe Register (www.gassaferegister.co.uk), which took over from CORGI as the official body for gas safety in the UK.

   As a landlord, you have a responsibility to ensure all your gas appliances are checked annually by a Gas Safe registered engineer, who will issue you with a gas safety certificate. If a tenant highlights an issue with a gas appliance, you need to have it fixed it within a reasonable amount of time. You could even have the appliances checked between tenancies, to show you really have tried your best to keep the tenant safe, although this is not necessarily a requirement. You must serve the gas safety certificate on the tenant before the start of the tenancy, otherwise this could prevent you from serving a valid Section 21 Notice. In the recent case of Caridon Property vs Monty Shooltz, the landlord's Section 21 case was dismissed because the gas safety certificate was not served on the tenant until after the tenancy started.

3. Electrical safety

The rules on electrical testing are not as straightforward as for gas safety but are soon to become clearer. You should do all you can to protect yourself and your tenants as much as possible and leave no room for doubt in anyone's mind that you have done the right thing. Poorly installed electrical fixtures have shown to be fire risks and, if something goes wrong and you can't demonstrate you took all reasonable steps to ensure the electrical installations were safe, you may be liable for losses incurred from fire... including loss of life.

The government announced in summer 2018 that it would be made mandatory for private landlords to ensure the electrics in their properties are inspected at least every five years. It is unlikely this will be a formal legal requirement for a while but you are recommended not to wait.

Electrical checks should be carried out by a qualified and competent electrical inspector to ensure they are up to the right standard. You should receive an Electrical Installation Condition Report (EICR) to give you and your tenants proof of the inspection.

Electrical work in homes in England and Wales needs to comply with Part P of the Building Regulations, so make sure you use a registered competent electrician. These tradespeople can self-certify their own work to demonstrate it meets Part P of the Building Regulations, saving you from having to arrange for local authority or other third-party certification. You can find a competent electrician at www.electricalcompetentperson.co.uk.

Rules in Scotland are different to those in England and Wales, with electrical work needing to comply with Scottish Building Standards, and certain larger electrical projects requiring a warrant. You should always check with your electrician to make sure you're taking the right precautions.

Some types of lets will require regular inspections, eg if you advertise student lets with an accommodation office, they may insist on annual inspections. HMOs must have an Electrical Installation Condition Report carried out at least every five years, with licensed HMOs often requiring further checks such as annual Portable Appliance Testing (PAT). I would advise at least an annual visual check, just to be on the safe side.

4. **Fire Safety**

Specific regulations for fire safety vary, depending on the type of property and let. With licensed HMOs, for example, landlords have a duty to provide access to clearly-signed fire exits, must install self-closing doors, fire extinguishers on each floor, a hardwired fire alarm system and need to have a fire risk-assessment form completed by an appropriate individual (preferably a Fire Safety Officer).

Fire safety rules on appliances in rented properties also vary from area to area, so to be 100% sure you're complying with the rules, contact your local authority's Environmental Health Officer and consult your local Fire Safety Officer.

5. **Heating**

The property obviously has to have a working heating system, which will be checked by either your Gas Safe engineer or your Part P registered electrician when they do their periodical certifications. Many tenancy agreements specify that the tenant must not use their own sources of heating (for example, oil and gas heaters), since you are unable to check whether they comply with safety rules and regulations but may still be liable if something goes wrong.

Of all the complaints and difficulties I come across between tenants and landlords, issues with heating are the most sensitive. Tenants who are cold will quickly stop paying the rent until the problem is sorted and if they're living in their own home for the first time, they often don't appreciate heating engineers aren't just sitting at home waiting for your call! So you have to explain the likely timescales of getting an engineer out, ordering parts and booking the work in.

If your tenant is vulnerable or elderly and it's during a particularly cold patch, make sure you get the heating fixed properly or do something (within the legals of letting) to help keep them warm in the meantime.

Also be aware that poor heating and ventilation are likely to lead to condensation, which can be a health hazard to tenants, damage their belongings and play havoc with your property. Make sure the property is properly heated and ventilated so that condensation doesn't become a source of irritation.

6. **Water**
The landlord usually takes responsibility for utility bills in an HMO, where tenant paying to rent a room rather than being responsible for the whole property. Typically room rents include all utility bills.

But if bills are not included in the rent, it is important the tenant has all the utilities in their own name, otherwise you can be liable for the bills if they don't pay.

Landlords letting properties in the Dwr Cymru Welsh Water (DCWW) and Dee Valley Water areas are legally obliged to provide the water company of the full name and date of birth of every occupant in a rented property, as well as the date the tenancy began.

There are plans to introduce similar legislation in England, under The Flood and Water Management Act 2010, although this has not yet been implemented. When the legislation comes into force, the property owner will be responsible for providing the tenant's details to the water supplier; if the owner fails to do this, they will become jointly responsibly with the tenant for any unpaid bills.

7. **Energy Efficiency**

    You are obliged to obtain an Energy Performance Certificate (EPC) for your rental property and give the tenant a copy of it before the start of the tenancy. The EPC rates the energy efficiency of a property on a scale from A to G (with A being the most efficient).

    Since 1st April 2018, landlords may no longer begin or renew a tenancy on any property which fails to meet the minimum energy efficiency standard (MEES) of E or higher, so it is important to improve the property's energy rating if it is currently F or G. And after 1st April 2023, you cannot continue to let any property with an EPC rating lower than E, unless an exemption has been granted.

    If you let to tenants on certain benefits, you may be able to secure funding to help with energy efficiency savings, through the government's Affordable Warmth scheme and as part of the government's Clean Growth Strategy, which was amended in April 2018. Find out more information here: www.gov.uk/energy-company-obligation. It's also worth checking with your energy provider as many of them offer free or discounted energy-saving home improvements from time to time.

    Separate legislation not connected to the MEES states that the landlord cannot refuse any reasonable request from a tenant to carry out energy efficiency improvements. It is, however, the tenant's responsibility to fund any work and landlords should not face any upfront costs, unless they agree. It may be possible for the work to be paid for through the tenant's energy bills under the government's Green Deal initiative (not available in Northern Ireland), although bear in mind the loan stays with the property when the tenant moves on, so both tenant and landlord must agree to the work. Find out more at gov.uk/greendeal.

The government is currently analysing feedback on its call for evidence on the current Green Deal Framework, so the scheme may be subject to change in the future.

8. **Make sure your tenant is given the prescribed information***
    Since the introduction of the Deregulation Act 2015, there has been certain prescribed information which you must provide to your tenant by law within 30 days of a new tenancy beginning. This includes:

    *   The property's Energy Performance Certificate (EPC)
    *   Gas safety certificate – before the tenant moves in. In a case from February 2018, a landlord failed to obtain a possession order because they had provided a copy of the gas safety certificate after the tenant had moved in
    *   A signed agreement to say they have confirmed there are working smoke and carbon monoxide detectors in the property
    *   A copy of the government's How to Rent guide
    *   Information relating to your chosen deposit protection scheme, including a receipt and the relevant scheme leaflet
    *   Any additional information required by your chosen deposit scheme – your scheme will be able to give you details.

*this is for England, so double check the requirements for Scotland, Wales and NI.

In addition, before a tenant moves in, it is worth giving them a verbal and/or written induction on all safety aspects. I would recommend having a folder in the property that contains written safety instructions/guidelines, copies of all the relevant certificates and clear instructions on what steps they should take if anything goes wrong, eg 'If there's a problem with the boiler, don't touch it, just call the landlord/agent on <number>' and emergency plumber details if there's a flood and you or your managing agent can't be contacted.

9. **Have issue and inspection logs**
    If you have a managing agent, they should be logging all complaints, problems and maintenance visits. If you're managing the property yourself, you need to set up a system for recording all complaints/issues, as described earlier in the chapter, and also for noting when checks have been carried out that are not part of the legal requirements. That would include things like extra gas and electrical checks between tenancies and regular fire alarm testing.

    Since October 2016, it has been a legal requirement in England to respond to any tenant repair requests within 14 days, so a log to track requests and responses is now essential if you are self-managing.

Who to work with

- Gas: Make sure an engineer is Gas Safe Registered – you can check at www.gassaferegister.co.uk
- Electrics: Employ a Part P Electrician – www.niceic.com, www.napit.org. uk, www.eca.co.uk and use either that electrician or another qualified PAT tester for your electrical appliances. You can find more information at pat-testing.info
- Energy Performance Certificates: find an assessor on epcregister.com

Hot Tip

SAVE MORE ENERGY: The Energy Saving Trust – EnergySavingTrust.org. uk – has a free advice line, which provides details about how you can save energy. It will keep you up to date with any changes to the Green Deal and give details of any grants that may be available to you for implementing energy-saving solutions.

Case Study

A case earlier this year was reported in the Evening Standard which involved a solicitor and her father being investigated by the police as the property they let in Edgware had a deadly carbon monoxide leak, which killed two men. Five other people were taken to hospital. The leak was suspected to come from a faulty boiler.

It was a truly tragic case.

Make sure ALL utilities are checked regularly and you are compliant and used qualified service engineers. The government are getting tough on landlords that don't comply – just watch the show I'm in on Channel 5, Bad Tenants, Rogue Landlords, and follow Harrow Council's enforcement team, both of which relate to unfit properties.

CHAPTER 11
WILL YOUR BUY-TO-LET WORK NOW?

I take calls every day from landlords who are about to go bust, so I know that buy-to-let success is not guaranteed at all. It's hard work and, no matter how well you prepare, things will occasionally go wrong.

Sometimes it's because you made a mistake, sometimes it won't be your fault at all but, either way, a problem can cost you thousands of pounds you hadn't planned to spend.

There are lots of reasons why people become buy-to-let landlords. Sometimes it's by accident, because they can't sell their home or they inherit a property and aren't sure what to do with it. Often it's a deliberate decision to try and accumulate extra income for retirement or to build a multi-million pound portfolio that they can sell in the future and retire early.

Whatever the reason for you becoming a landlord, for your buy-to-let to work now you must make sure the properties you have already bought or inherited and those you are going to buy stack up financially. And for that to happen, you need to be clear on what your financial objectives are and make sure you understand the core buy-to-let financial calculations.

Taxes

There have been some significant changes to landlord taxation in the past few years. The main taxes you will have to pay are:

Stamp duty land tax (England)
Stamp duty (SDLT) saw a significant hike for buyers of second homes in April 2016. If you already own a property – and this includes your home –

you will pay an additional 3% in stamp duty on the full purchase price over the property value of £40,000, further eating into your profit, although this is tax deductible on sale.

For example, a £150,000 property would previously have incurred the same stamp duty charge, regardless of whether it was a second home. There are now three tiers of stamp duty for a property of this price:

- First-time buyer - £0
- Home-mover or buyer who has owned property before - £500
- Investor (who already owns at least one property) - £5,000

Scotland and Wales
Stamp duty has been replaced with land and buildings transaction tax (LBTT) in Scotland and by land transaction tax (LTT) in Wales. These both operate in a similar way to stamp duty but with different bands and rates. The 3% surcharge still applies for second homes.

You can calculate LTT payable in Wales here: www.beta.gov.wales/land-transaction-tax-calculator

The LBTT rates for Scotland can be calculated here: www.stampdutycalculator.org.uk/stamp-duty-scotland.htm

Income tax
From April 2017, the government began phasing in Section 24, which restricts the amount of income tax relief landlords can claim on residential property finance costs. Previously, you could offset all of your mortgage interest payments – as well as interest on loans for furnishings – against your income, at your usual tax rate.

Michael Wright, of RITA4Rent, explains: "Under the new system, the profit you are taxed on is artificially inflated because, by 2020 when the new rules are fully in place, mortgage interest and finance costs will no longer form part of your property expenses. This tax is reduced by an amount typically equating to your mortgage interest multiplied by 20%.

"You will continue to be able to offset all your other expenses, such as insurances, repairs, letting agent fees, accountancy fees, mileage, costs of office, etc."

This example shows how taxable profit was calculated in the past:

Rental income	£10,000
Rental costs (not including mortgage interest)	£1,000
Mortgage interest	£6,000
Taxable profit	**£3,000**

Up to and including the tax year 2016/17, you would only be taxed on the profit, ie £3,000. But this changes dramatically as Section 24 is phased in and only a 20% tax credit is available, regardless of your current tax bracket.

This means if £6,000 of the rental costs are on mortgage interest, you will eventually be taxed on all of that amount, too.

Tax year	Interest relief	Interest taxable	Taxable profit
2016/17	100%	£0	£3,000
2017/18	75%	£1,500	£4,500
2018/19	50%	£3,000	£6,000
2019/20	25%	£4,500	£7,500
2020/21	0%	£6,000	£9,000

Michael added: "To confirm, in the 20/21 tax year above, your profit will be artificially higher to the value of £6,000 compared to the 16/17 year under the old rules. The tax calculated is then reduced by an amount typically equating to your mortgage interest, multiplied by 20%."

You are most likely to suffer under the new rules if you are a higher rate tax-payer, or if your new "higher" earnings (on paper at least) will push you up into the next tax bracket. If you have mortgaged properties, I recommend you seek expert advice from a tax specialist who understands property.

Replacement Domestic Item relief

This is a new tax relief introduced in April 2016 to replace the old wear and tear allowance, which applied to furnished properties only.

Replacement Domestic Item relief is available on all rental properties, furnished or unfurnished, and applies to things such as fridges, cookers, furnishings – eg carpets and curtains – and any furniture or kitchenware you supply.

You cannot claim tax relief on the initial purchase of these items when setting up the property, but can claim for the expense of replacing them when necessary.

You can only claim for 'like for like' replacements, and not for upgrades. For example, if you replace a small under-counter fridge (which would cost around £170) with a fridge-freezer costing £270, you can only claim tax relief on the first £170, as the rest of the expense is considered an upgrade.

You could, however, claim for any costs incurred when disposing of the old fridge, minus any money you may receive for it.

Capital Gains tax

If you bought a property in 2000 for £50,000 and it's worth £100,000 today, the capital growth is £50,000.

Tax on capital growth is treated differently to income tax and can be complicated to calculate, so you must seek specialist tax advice for your own circumstances. But an important point to remember, which too many people get wrong, is that you're taxed on the increase on your purchase price, not the equity. So, if you buy at £200,000, remortgage at a later date and pull out £40,000, then eventually sell at £300,000, you will be taxed on the full £100,000 increase in value (minus tax deductions), not just the remaining £60,000 equity that you realise when you sell.

Key steps

1. **Clarify what you're trying to achieve with your investment.**
    Fundamentally, you must know what financial returns you want from your portfolio investment and by when. What would you like your portfolio to be worth in the future? How much equity do you intend to have in the portfolio by then? What rental income do you want to be achieving on a monthly basis from each property? Are you more concerned with rental income or capital growth? These decisions will impact everything about your investment: what and where you buy, how you rent the property, the kind of mortgage you get and the amount of capital you invest into the property.

    For example, if you want to take an income, ideally you want to have a low loan to value and may choose a higher income rental option with a higher risk profile tenant, such as an HMO. If you simply want a lump sum in the future, you may not be worried so much about paying off the mortgage and take a high loan-to-value mortgage on an interest-only basis, letting the property to easy-to-manage tenants. In that case, you will also be more concerned about planning for how to sell off each property to minimise the tax implications.

2. **Make sure you understand yield and capital growth**
    These are two of the main key performance indicators used by buy-to-let landlords.

Yield: I spoke about this briefly in Chapter 4. Calculating a property's yield will allow you to compare one property with another to see which could generate the best financial return. It can also give you a broad indication of how the property investment stacks up against other financial investments, such as stocks and shares.

Yield is calculated in a number of different ways, but is typically the rental income divided by the property value:

Property value: £100,000
Rental income: £10,000 = 10% Gross Yield

Rental costs: £7,000
Net income: £3,000 = 3% Net Yield

Don't forget that the £3,000 may be taxed as income, so you need to work out your net amount after tax

And bear in mind that yield is not the same as your return, which is broadly calculated according to the amount of capital you invest, ie your deposit and funds invested for refurbishment.

ROCI = profit ÷ capital invested, eg

Total capital invested £50,000
Annual gross profit £20,000 = 40% ROCI
Annual net profit £7,000 = 14% ROCI

Two investors could have the same gross yield, but if one is highly leveraged and one owns the property outright, their profit figures, net yield and return on capital invested will be significantly different.

Capital growth: Capital growth is the increase in the value of your property or portfolio, as explained above.

From 2000, many homeowners and lots of property investors were making more money from the growth in the value of their home than they were from their salary. From 2007, though, prices went crashing down and landlords who kept borrowing and borrowing to buy more properties suddenly found themselves with little – if any – equity left in their portfolio. When rents went down in 2008, some of these landlords found the rental income wasn't covering their costs either and had their properties repossessed.

To avoid this happening to you, it's wise to make sure you always have at least 25% equity. Landlords who have got into difficulty in recent years have tended to be the ones that only put a 5% or 10% deposit down or went for 'no money down' deals. If you're going to leverage very highly, the property needs to be generating a very good profit and, even then, these landlords often end up with financial problems at some point.

If you want to secure some capital growth as well as income, the best strategy is to build in some equity from the start, by renovating, extending or buying a property from a distressed seller who is able to sell it to you at a bargain price.

3. **Work out the 'rental ratio'**
   To reinforce what I said in Chapter 4, you need to be sure that you can get a mortgage for a property before you start making offers. Lenders will expect the rent to cover mortgage repayments and the cost of any additional borrowing against the property by 125%-145%. For example, if the mortgage payments are going to be £500 per month, the property will need to generate £625-£725 rent a month for the mortgage company to agree to lend you the money.

Who to work with

There are various experts you need to help you work out the potential returns from a buy-to-let property and your portfolio as a whole.

Letting agents

A good, proactive letting agent should understand all the costs involved in buy-to-let and be able to help you work out whether a property or your portfolio stacks up financially. They will know the rental income each type of let is currently achieving and they'll also know what each type of tenant is looking for. Ask local letting agents what kind of property is always in great demand and short supply and then you can fill that demand. Make sure you choose an agent who has Client Money Protection, as this will soon be a legal requirement, and one who is well prepared for the upcoming lettings fee ban and regulation. Self-regulated agents who are members of a trade association are most likely to survive these changes over the next few years.

Specialist mortgage lenders

Lenders and brokers who have a great deal of experience in buy-to-let will have their own methods of checking whether a property will give you a healthy enough return to make sure you can make the mortgage payments!

Buy-to-let consultants

There are loads of 'gurus' out there who say they can tell you which are the right properties to invest in. Unfortunately, many of them are also trying to sell you properties they have a vested interest in selling, or courses costing thousands of pounds. In my opinion, that means they are not likely to be as impartial as you need them to be. Ideally, you should spend your time and money learning how to assess a property for yourself, but there are some consultants who can help you.

Wealth and tax advisers

In my experience, buy-to-let investors rarely give enough consideration to their tax position or take enough time to consult experts on their full financial circumstances. This is a major mistake. The right tax and wealth planning advice can make the difference between a reasonable investment and an excellent one. Too many landlords only find out when it's too late that their portfolio is only going to provide them with a fraction of the financial security that they expected.

Before you add a property to your existing assets (for example, your own business, your home or shares and investments you have), you need to understand the tax implications on your current circumstances.

Wealth and tax experts who already work with buy-to-let companies and landlords will be able to really help you work out the best way to invest.

Questions to ask

Apart from checking that any expert you work with has the appropriate qualifications and certifications, it's wise to ask:

- How long have they been working with buy-to-let clients?
- Are they happy to put you in touch with at least 3 satisfied clients?
- Do they invest in property themselves and are they investing in the current market?
- What insurance can they offer in case HMRC decide to investigate you?
- Have they ever won a battle with HMRC?

Hot Tip

MAKE IT VISUAL: Get a fold-out map of the local area and as you do your research about which areas and roads are in demand. You can highlight where to focus your property hunt and which areas to avoid. It's useful for you and very useful to take in to show agents!

CHAPTER 12
WILL YOUR BUY-TO-LET WORK IN THE FUTURE?

Most buy-to-let investors put some effort into calculating whether a property stacks up in today's market. Few spend time considering how the investment will be in the future. For example, imagine you'd bought a property in Cardiff or Leeds 20 years ago. If you'd known then what those cities would be like today, you'd probably have bought something very different.

Although we can't predict the future with 100% accuracy, plans for an area are often set 10-20 years in advance, so it is possible to have some idea of what a place is going to look like.

Fundamentally, if you want to make money from an investment, demand needs to exceed supply. For example, if there are four tenants chasing one property, the rent will typically go up. If two buyers have five properties to choose from, they will offer below the asking prices and are likely to bag a bargain.

So the trick to investing in a property that stacks up now and in the future is to find property types and areas that are always going to be in short supply, either from a rental or purchase demand perspective... and preferably both!

Key steps

1. Assess future demand & supply
Areas tend to become more popular and therefore grow in value with transport improvements, like a new train or tram station or new bypass and business and amenities developments. Look out for developers entering the area, improvements to shopping centres, businesses expanding or relocating and new attractions, eg the O2 Centre in Greenwich.

But bear in mind that regeneration can sometimes result in an oversupply of certain types of properties, as happened with new build flats in many cities around the UK.

At Nottingham's Marco Island, for example, some apartments have been sold for half their original price. One listed on Rightmove, purchased new at £93,500 in 2005, was sold in 2012 for just £58,500. Prices have still not recovered; at the time of print, one sold in March 2017 at £79,000, having previously been sold for £114,750 in January 2006

This is by no means a unique situation. A BBC study in October 2017 discovered that properties in 58% of wards in England and Wales were selling for less than they were in 2007, when you take inflation into account.

So you not only need to understand which areas and properties will be attractive to people in the future, but also the likely level of increase (or decrease) of the population and therefore the number of people looking for a home.

2. **Track your investment returns**
    Whether you're only buying one or two properties to let or are running a larger portfolio, you need to check regularly how well your property is performing against your investment objectives.

    For buy-to-let investment, you need tenants to rent your property and for that rent to grow at least as much as inflation on an annual basis. Over the last 10 years, on average, private rents have risen by 2% per year versus 2.7% inflation (Source: ONS). If your rent isn't keeping up with inflation and you hope to secure income from your portfolio in the future, you're likely to fall short of your target.

    For example, the £1,000 a month net rent you're assuming will boost your pension might only be worth £500 by the time you come to retire.

And from a capital growth perspective, you really want your property portfolio to out-perform the average growth for the local area. If your property is only keeping up with the average, it's likely you could find other property investments that will stack up better financially.

Who to work with

You can check future infrastructure plans with your local council planners and by studying the area's Local Plan. Everyone has the right of access to see what transport and development changes are currently planned and you can also see what kind of planning applications have been submitted by house-builders.

Use the UK House Price Index (HPI) to check average changes over the last 12 months for your area and type of property, then check the sold house price data on Rightmove for similar properties to yours, both now and 12 months ago, and you'll get a picture of how your investment is performing against the local average.

Questions to ask

To summarise, you need to ask:

- What's going on in the local infrastructure that's likely to affect the future supply and demand for my type of investment?
- What type of property, in which location is most likely to be consistently in demand in the future?
- Is my rental income at least keeping up with inflation?
- Is my investment beating or just keeping up with average growth for my area?
- Based on all the above, am I investing in the right thing, or should I think about switching to a different kind of property?

....

Hot Tip

PRICES GO DOWN AS WELL AS UP: Whatever you buy or own (including your personal home), make sure you research what changes are likely to happen in the area and don't forget that some things can reduce the value of a property too, such as a telephone mast being built nearby or a council waste dump. Make sure you can afford the property whether prices rise or fall, so you sell when you want to and aren't forced to sell at a loss.

PART TWO
LETTING YOUR PROPERTY

CHAPTER 13
SHOULD I USE A LETTING AGENT?

I always recommend you use a letting/managing agent to manage your property. As a landlord, do you want to be taking calls in the early hours of the morning from a tenant whose boiler has broken down? Or a 5am call from a drunk tenant who has lost their keys? My preference would be for a managing agent to sort that for me, depending on my time and my lifestyle.

According to the Council of Mortgage Lenders (now UK Finance), over 60% of landlords have just one property and most landlords are also in full-time employment. If you pay a letting/management fee, the agent will then

- find you a tenant
- sustain the tenancy
- deal with inventories
- deal with your paperwork
- collect tenants' payments
- sort out gas and electrical checks
- deal with maintenance issues
- deal with all the necessary rules and regulations and compliance issues

It's a bit of a no-brainer!

As a landlord, always put a price on your time and remember: **cheap can turn out to be expensive**

Currently anyone can set up to be a letting agent but since October 2014 all letting agents have had to belong to a redress scheme; in 2017 the Property Redress Scheme made 360 decisions after adjudication on complaints about letting agents.

The government now want tenants to have a better offering from landlords and letting agents and has committed to making letting agents regulated in the future, which means letting agents will have to:

1. be part of a redress scheme
2. have professional indemnity insurance
3. have Client Money Protection
4. have some basic training even, if they do not belong to a trade association

On the whole, letting agents give a great service but those letting in England are now entering unprecedented challenging times with the introduction of the Tenant Fees Bill, which prohibits them from charging any administration fees to tenants. This is expected to become law in April 2019.

My personal opinion is that I don't think letting agents will increase their fees to landlords as their focus will be on retaining their existing landlords and attracting new ones in a very competitive market. It does mean landlords will be in a strong position to shop around for the agent providing the best quality of service at the right price.

The Tenant Fees Bill will also restrict holding deposits to no more than one week's rent, and deposits at the start of a tenancy to no more than six weeks' rent.

Before you decide you don't need the services of a letting agent, be warned! I am contacted with issues *far* more often by landlords who don't use letting agents than by those who do. Landlords who manage properties and tenants themselves often miss rental payments, don't react quickly enough when tenants don't pay their rent, can't always respond quickly enough to maintenance issues and often issue the wrong paperwork when they try to evict a tenant.

As a landlord, you need to be honest with yourself as to whether you can dedicate the time, resources and effort to run a buy-to-let portfolio legally and effectively. If you don't want to spend hours every week keeping up to date with landlord legals, local authority rules and regulations, tenant payments, inventories, gas and electrical checks, fire alarm testing and all the paperwork that goes with letting a property, then a letting agent may actually save you money in the long run.

Key steps

1. **DIY?**
   Really think about not just whether you *can*, but also whether you *want* to let and manage your properties yourself. Do you know all the steps you should be taking to ensure you comply with the law? Are you willing to take calls from tenants at all times of the day (and possibly night) and can you handle co-ordinating all the maintenance?

2. **What's your time worth?**
   Lots of landlords make the mistake of not putting a value on their own time. They think they're saving money by managing their portfolio themselves, but all the time they spend doing that is time they're not getting paid for. Look at your hourly rate and calculate how much time you'd be spending every month managing your properties. Is it really worth your while? In my experience, in many cases it's a false economy.

3. **Pick the right agent**
   As with picking an agent to sell your property, you need to pick a letting agent who is already successfully letting properties like yours. The most common complaints I get about agents are that the agent has kept the rent and not passed it on, they didn't protect the deposit in the scheme or they have given a poor management service, so it's incredibly important you engage the right agent who will help maximise the profitability of your investment.

Who to work with

Make sure your letting agent belongs to a government-approved redress scheme, which has been a legal requirement since October 2014. The schemes are The Property Ombudsman, and The Property Redress Scheme, on whose Advisory Committee I sit.

This legislation ensures that if a landlord or tenant has a complaint against an agent they can't resolve, they can go to the relevant scheme provider and the complaint can be dealt with by an independent third party, free of charge. An award can be made against the agent for their conduct. If a member is expelled but carries on practising, the local authority can issue a fine of £5,000.

You should always make sure that, in addition to being a member of a redress scheme, an agent has Client Money Protection (CMP) Insurance in place, so that your rent and tenants' deposits are covered if the company goes bust. This will be a legal requirement from the 1st April 2019. Agents should also belong to a trade association as a bare minimum, as these agents are most likely to pass regulatory requirements in the future.

Letting agents typically charge you a set-up fee and a percentage of the rent they collect for you (between 5% and 15%) on a monthly basis. They will also charge for certificates, such as EPCs, gas safety and electrical safety. I tend to find that if they charge a low commission rate, they normally charge you a higher set-up fee or more for EPCs or certificates, so most end up charging the same overall.

One piece of good news for you is that letting agent fees are all tax deductible, so the actual amount you pay if your property is cash-flow positive is less than the amount you pay net of tax.

The government has committed to regulating letting agents in the future, so the better agent you choose now, the more likely they are to survive the changes over the next few years. Choosing an agent that does not work to the highest standards may result in issues with your tenant and rent payments in the future.

Questions to ask

1. You don't want a letting agent who just rents property for you. You want one who understands the buy-to-let process from start to finish. Do they know which properties or areas give the best yields or produce the best capital growth?
2. How do they keep up with national and local lettings rules and regulations?
3. What would happen if they went bust or someone ran off with the rent?
4. How would they help you if a tenant went into arrears?
5. What checks do they make on the property to ensure there is no damage by tenants?
6. How will they handle any complaints you might have?
7. How much does the tenant pay in administration charges to rent a property from the agent? (These fees are expected to be banned in April 2019).
8. What happens if there is a disagreement over the inventory?
9. What are all their on-going fees and charges, for example, do they charge to re-let a property to the same tenant? All agents, by law, have to provide you with all of their fees.
10. What insurances and guarantees come with any maintenance work they carry out?

Hot Tip

DOUBLE-CHECK THE REFERENCING: Check how the letting agent references tenants. If they only use online credit checks, this is unlikely, in my experience, to be good enough to ensure you have a tenant who will always pay their rent.

Case Study

I always recommend landlords use a letting agent, but over the years I have come across rogues, that will take the rent and not pass it on to the landlord.

A case I was involved with featured Carter Stones in Ilford, where there were numerous landlords affected, who were victims of unlawful subletting. The agent was subsequently expelled by the Property Redress Scheme and has since closed down. It was a nightmare situation; they even locked me in their office while we were filming for Channel 5's Nightmare Tenants, Slum Landlords.

I will always try to expose a rogue agent because they give the industry a bad name and tarnish the good ones. Regulation of letting agents will be coming in and the best news was that Client Money Protection is to become mandatory from 1st April 2019. This means that the agent will have to have this insurance in place, or face a fine of up to £30k. So when you look to instruct an agent, after doing your due diligence on them, ask if they belong to a redress scheme, if they have Professional Indemnity Insurance and if

Client Money Protection is in place. It's A MUST.

HAMILTON FRASER

TOTAL
LANDLORD
INSURANCE

Positively Perfect Property Protection

We're not perfect but... we have once again been voted as the **'Best Landlord Insurance Provider'** by UK customers in the annual Insurance Choice Awards.

To obtain 'positively perfect protection' call 0800 63 43 880

CHAPTER 14
BUY-TO-LET INSURANCE

It's essential to buy the correct insurances.

There are certain types of insurance you must have, while others are optional, but I'd advise you to consider taking out most of them. In my view, not spending money on insurance to cover the risks of buy-to-let is a false economy. For example, the cost of a tenant who isn't paying any rent is likely to run into thousands of pounds, whereas insurance for this would only cost a couple of hundred pounds.

Whatever insurance you take out, make sure it's from companies who understand buy-to-let and the specific risks of renting out a property. I have had people come to me who have taken out standard buildings and contents insurance and then found out that they aren't covered for malicious damage, which can cost tens of thousands. So make sure you're clear on what your insurance covers and, more importantly, what it might *not* cover.

Key steps

1. **Understand which insurance policies are essential**
   You may be required by your lender to take out buildings insurance (and possibly other insurance) as a condition of the mortgage, so make sure you understand what is required and exactly what it covers you for. If you have a buy-to-let mortgage, you're likely to need a specialist landlord policy that covers you for problems tenants can cause.

2. **Take out specialist landlord buildings and contents insurance**
   Even if you don't have a mortgage, or your lender doesn't require you to have insurance as a condition of your mortgage, every landlord should take out specialist buildings and contents insurance as a bare

minimum. A standard policy will cover you for damage to the property itself, such as fire or flood (typically from a leak), but as a landlord you need insurance that covers your property for damage a tenant could cause, either accidentally or on purpose. Ordinary insurance will only cover the owner for this type of risk.

Most landlord-specific policies also include, or offer as an option:

- Legal cover
- Loss of rent cover, eg if the property is damaged so much the tenant can't live there
- Public liability and property owners' insurance: this will cover you if a tenant, guest or contractor is injured due to a problem with your property.

3. **Consider other insurance policies**
    These are down to your personal choice, but really think about whether they represent value for money to you. I would suggest they are all seriously worth considering.

    Rent guarantees and warranties: There are various types and I think some are extremely expensive, so take time to research what's available and how much it costs. You may decide it's better just to keep some money aside to cover your costs should your property be empty for any reason or your tenant decides not to pay the rent.

    These are the different types of policies currently available:

    - **Deposit protection**: This allows a tenant to move in without a deposit, but protects you against any damage and unpaid rent.
    - **Section 21 protection**: Without cover, issuing a Section 21 to your tenant will cost you several hundred pounds – or even thousands if it's a complicated case. But if you buy cover, instead of *you* funding my fees to issue the Section 21, the insurance will pay me to do it for you!

- **Rental protection**: Not having any rent coming in and spending hundreds or thousands of pounds covering your costs and, potentially, legal disputes with tenants will make a serious dent in your cash flow. This insurance means you can still get your rent paid and some policies guarantee you'll receive it on the same day as you would normally every month. The downside is that it can be expensive, so you need to weigh up the costs versus the risk. Also, it's very important to make sure you're not buying legal cover twice, eg through buildings and contents and this type of insurance policy.

Emergency cover: Some landlords don't mind being called out at inconvenient times to sort out boilers failing or pipes leaking. But if you aren't keen to deal with these issues and don't have good electric and plumbing/heating suppliers who will drop everything to go to your property, it's worth looking at the pros and cons of investing in emergency cover insurance.

4. Think about life cover

As an investor, it's worth looking at some form of life cover, particularly if you own multiple properties and have some in joint names, with a business partner or spouse. I would also suggest you take advice from a financial specialist rather than buying 'off the shelf' cover.

The aim of the cover is to ensure that if something happens to you, the other person receives enough money to maintain the property portfolio and pay off any potential inheritance tax money due.

5. Do all you can to avoid a stressful claims process

A good insurance company will make life easy for you when it comes to a claim. But there are things you need to do in order to help them:

- Keep records in order – for example, the tenancy agreement, any communication with the tenant, dates and times of problems that have occurred and what you have done about it, as well as guarantees by tradespeople for their work.

- Make sure you keep your payments up to date. There is nothing worse than not renewing a policy, only to have problems a few days after your cover has expired!
- Ring the insurer before you call anyone else. Many insurers have their own 'contacts' they will want you to use.

Who to work with

Double-check that any company offering you insurance is a member of the Financial Conduct Authority (FCA), as they are required to be. That means they are regulated and you have a redress scheme via the Financial Ombudsman Service if you have any issues with your insurer.

Try also to work with an insurer who is a member of the Association of British Insurers (ABI) and the broker needs to be FCA authorised, as they have various Codes of Practice and Best Practice Guidelines set out for their members.

Questions to ask

There are three very important questions you must be able to answer:

1. **Does your insurance cover you for typical landlord and tenant issues?**
   Any insurance company can create a policy and call it 'landlord insurance'; however, cheap policies typically will give you less cover than more expensive ones.

   The reason you want insurance is to cover yourself from the risks to you (and your family and finances) of letting a property. You need to decide what risks would keep you up at night and what risks would mean you end up losing your property due to costs you could incur through no fault of your own.

In my experience, these are the top five problems landlords experience while letting a property:

- Tenants not paying their rent.
- Boilers breaking down, water leaks and plumbing or drainage problems.
- Tenants damaging the property, eg maliciously, because you're trying to evict them.
- Tenants not setting aside enough of their Local Housing Allowance/Universal Credit to pay the rent, or having their benefits suspended/reduced at short notice
- Professional gangs setting up cannabis factories.

2. Are you clear on what you are covered for – and not?
All insurers will have specific risks they will exclude from their policy, depending on their experience and knowledge of lettings risks.

For example, some policies will not cover tenants who are on housing benefit or students. Bear in mind you may take on a tenant in employment who is then made redundant and becomes reliant on benefits. In this case, you need to review your insurance. I have also come across cases whereby unspent criminal convictions can void the insurance policy, so if you don't reference check the tenant in the way the insurance policy requires, you may end up not being covered.

3. Do you understand your obligations to the insurance company?
Insurers normally have requirements that they expect you to adhere to – and if you don't, they may not pay out on your claim.

For example, you have an obligation to maintain the property properly, so if you don't keep drains and guttering freely flowing or update a water tank when you should and leaks or a flood occur, you may not get the payout you expect. Also, be aware that the insurance company may require you to include certain clauses in your tenancy agreement.

Finally, it is now mandatory to disclose levels of commission, if asked, so do ask the insurance broker what commission they earn from selling the policy. This will help you compare different policies and decide whether you're getting value for money.

Recommended: www.totallandlordinsurance.co.uk

Hot Tip

INSURE FROM EXCHANGE: Make sure you insure the property from the time you take ownership – ie at exchange of contracts – don't wait until you get a tenant in.

Case Study

As you may know, I'm Brand Ambassador for Hamilton Fraser and one of our brands is Total Landlord Insurance. Our claims team told me of a very strange and grim story.

The landlord client who took out the insurance policy was contacted by the police to say there had been a murder at the rear of his rented property and a body found under the back garden.

When they went in to arrest the two men at the property, they found a cannabis factory. There was building damage, including smashed walls. The electrics had been rewired, the water system rerouted and chimney blocked.

Thankfully because he had landlord insurance he was able to claim £17,362.

CHAPTER 15
WORKING OUT THE RENT

Rents can go up and down on a month-by-month basis, depending on what's happening in the market. Working out what the rent is when you're first researching the property is one thing, but you also need to review the rent you're charging on a three to six-month basis, to make sure you're maximising your earnings.

That doesn't necessarily mean increasing the rent, it may actually mean slightly reducing it, to ensure your property is rented out and not sitting empty. Empty properties are a landlord's worst nightmare.

Voids: the cash flow killer!
For a landlord, apart from having your property trashed or a tenant not paying, the next worst thing is a property without a tenant. If you can rent a property for £500 a month, every empty day costs around £16 in lost revenue!

Letting agents despair at landlords who would rather have such a property stand empty for a month than let it at £475 (effectively costing around 80p a day instead of £16). As a landlord, you have to think like a businessperson: cash is king and choosing to leave your product/service unsold, rather than let it go for a fraction less than you would do normally, could easily result in you going bust. You still have to pay the bills associated with the property – mortgage, maintenance, possibly utilities, etc – so not only are you not losing income, it's actually costing you money to subsidise your investment. Voids can very quickly turn your asset into a liability.

Key steps

1. **Budget for voids**

   While you're still at the initial planning stage, bear in mind that professional landlords budget for three to four weeks (ie a full month's void) a year for times when the property is not earning rent. This allows for refurbishment or for the few days you typically need between tenants to clean, carry out inspections and make any repairs/changes prior to the property being re-let.

   Factor this into your figures and make sure the investment still stacks up for you.

2. **Check out the competition**

   Go online and see how much properties similar to yours are being advertised for. When you're searching on property portals, always tick the 'let' box so you know which properties are actually being rented, otherwise you're in danger of basing your rent on ones that may be advertised at too high a price and are sitting empty.

3. **Talk to local letting agents**

   Ask the experts what makes the difference between a property being let within days or taking weeks or months to rent. Once you have an idea of what bracket your property will be advertised in, visit other properties available for the same level of rent, check their location and condition and make sure your property is better!

Questions to ask

1. **What is the realistic rent you will receive?**

   It's vital that you're as certain as it's possible to be about how much rent you'll get. If you don't do your research properly, you could end up with an investment that doesn't stack up as you want or need.

Unfortunately, you can't control the market forces! For example, if you want a gross yield of 7%, and have planned on getting £600 per month rent to secure that 7%, but the market says it's only worth £500, suddenly then that's what it is worth. So, again, when you're doing your research, allow for a fluctuation in market values. Of course, it's ideal if the rent you can charge is above your ideal yield, so even if rents fall, you're still on target.

2. **Where are you getting your rental advice from?**
   If the average monthly rental figure is being given by companies or individuals who are also trying to sell you a property, ignore it! Advice from someone who makes their money from selling something to you isn't anywhere near as good as advice from someone who's independent and has no vested interest in what you do. You can get independent rental averages from RICS surveyors and any letting agent that purely rents properties.

3. **Will your rent keep up with inflation?**
   Rents typically keep up with wage inflation, so if wages go up by 2% locally, then this allows rents to do the same. Depending on demand and supply, sometimes rents can grow above inflation. More often than not, though, they tend to lag behind. As discussed in Chapter 12, it's an important measure to track if you're investing for a pension income long term, as rents which don't keep up with the cost of living can erode the real value of your future rental income.

   For example, if your rents stay the same, while inflation runs at 5%, then your rent will buy you 5% less each year. You can find the latest rental prices here:

   www.ons.gov.uk/economy/inflationandpriceindices/bulletins/indexof privatehousingrentalprices/previousReleases

Hot Tip

PRICE RIGHT: Set your rent at a level slightly below other competitors' properties. Providing your property is well maintained, it will always be one of the first let and voids will be kept to a minimum.

CHAPTER 16
ADVERTISING YOUR BUY-TO-LET

Every day that your property is not let it's costing you money, so it's imperative that it is advertised at the right time and in the right way. You need to make sure it's being promoted to your target tenants well enough in advance of the target move-in date so it's empty for as little time as possible.

When to advertise
If the property doesn't require any refurbishment, aim to start advertising as soon as you've exchanged contracts. Legally, at this point you're responsible for the property so, providing the people you are buying from agree, or if it's already vacant, then you (or your letting agent) should be able to show prospective tenants around.

If you have a good, proactive agent, and/or you advertise your property in the right areas, then you should be able to start earning rental income from your property on the day you complete.

If you're refurbishing, start advertising as soon as the property site is at a safe stage – often tenants like the idea that they'll be the first ones in a newly-updated property. And if you already have a tenant in the property, then there should be a clause in the contract allowing you to show prospective tenants once the existing tenants have entered their notice period.

Where to advertise
If you're letting through an agent, it should be their responsibility to advertise the property for rent and conduct the viewings. As a minimum, your property should be advertised on the main property portals, such as Rightmove, OnTheMarket and Zoopla, as well as any well-known local rental portals. If you're planning to self-manage, it's also worth looking at Upad, OpenRent, Urban.co.uk, No Agent and LettingaProperty.com. Increasingly, tenants are finding property via the internet, rather than through newspaper advertising,

but this can vary from area to area, particularly if you're renting rooms, so carry out some local research as to what works best.

Viewings
A viewing is the written advert brought to life, so you need to make sure it comes up to scratch! Whether you're letting the property yourself or via an agent, it's worth going on the first few viewings yourself to make sure there are no 'hiccups', eg the tenant/owner of the property is telling you it's fine to have tenants viewing but the letting agent is telling you they can't get in or the place is a mess when it's too late!

It's important to be aware of current legislation; for example, an Energy Performance Certificate must be available to show to prospective tenants. Ideally, also have the latest gas and electrical safety certificates too and advise the tenant which company you (or your agent) will use to protect their deposit.

Making sure you have all of these things available at the time of viewing helps promote you as a good landlord that lets property legally, as opposed to a rogue that is unlikely to bother with checks and deposit protection.

If you have the misfortune to have a bad tenant, who you're in the process of evicting, they will probably refuse you access. In this case, you can't simply let yourself in, as that would be deemed harassment; you may just have to wait until the tenant has left before you can carry out viewings. It's a real headache for landlords and very frustrating, but you must make sure you stay on the right side of the law.

While you may not refuse to let to somebody based on their race, religion/belief, sex/gender, sexual orientation or disability under the Equality Act 2010, you may still see private ads – and even those from letting agents – saying 'no DSS' or 'no social tenants'. This is not advised as, even though being in receipt of benefits is not a protected characteristic, it could be considered discrimination, especially in the light of a high profile case which drew attention to this issue in early 2018.

A single mother challenged a letting agency which refused to let to her because she was on benefits, despite her 11-year record of paying rent on time. She successfully argued that single women are more likely to claim housing benefit than single men, so the policy was an example of indirect discrimination. The agency admitted this and awarded her compensation.

However, because the case was settled out of court, no legal precedent has been set, which means this is still something of a grey area.

Key steps

1. **Make sure viewings can be carried out!**
   This might sound like an odd thing to say, but before you advertise, make sure you have something in writing (if not already in the contract) from the current property owner or your existing tenants, confirming they will allow viewings and will make sure the property is well presented. Agree how often and at what times prospective tenants can be shown around.

2. **Prepare your advertisement correctly**
   One thing to bear in mind if you're advertising yourself or not using a self-regulated letting agent is that the description you give of the property must adhere to the new rules that mean letting agents and landlords have joint responsibility for the accuracy of property descriptions. It is an offence to make untrue statements about a property.

   For example, if a property has three rooms you're using as bedrooms, but one of them is a loft room, which hasn't been passed by building regulations as a bedroom, then the property should be advertised as 'two bedrooms with a loft room'. If your property details aren't accurate, the tenant could sue you, cancel the tenancy and may even be able to claim back all the rent they've paid!

Checklist of what to include in the property advert:

- Several high-quality photographs
- Location
- Style of property (modern, new build, Victorian, warehouse, etc)
- Standard features (rooms, central heating, garage, etc)
- Proximity to shops, schools, transport infrastructure, etc
- Furnished or unfurnished
- What tenants would be suitable, eg professional couple.

Note: you may want to consider offering the property to smokers and pet owners to widen your market.

- Desired rent (per week or per month)
- Whether bills are included
- Contact details
- If you don't want agents calling you up, specify 'NO AGENTS'

3. Advertise in the right places

Depending on your type of let and target tenant, different media will work better. Do some local research to find out which is better for you, eg if you're renting rooms to professionals, Spareroom and Easyroommate might work best; if you're renting to students or casual workers, Gumtree, www.studentaccomodation.co.uk, local papers and postcards in shops might be more effective; if you're renting to couples or families, Rightmove may be the best.

On the main property portals, it's usually worth upgrading to take an enhanced listing, to make sure your property is highlighted and appears as far up the listings as possible. The day you list your property is important; James Davis at Upad reports that Monday is the best day of the week to advertise, with response rates decreasing throughout the week. He also says more than 60% of tenants set up alerts from property portals, and a third of enquiries are received within 48 hours of a listing appearing.

4. Carry out the viewing in the right way

First make sure you have everything to hand, in terms of certificates and information about the property, to show the prospective tenant you are letting legally:

1. The EPC
2. A copy of the latest gas and electrical safety certificates
3. Information about how their deposit will be held in the Tenancy Deposit Scheme for their protection.

Secondly, try to find out more about the person viewing so you can get an idea of their situation and lifestyle and what kind of tenant they might be. Ask them questions such as:

1. Are they employed?
2. Where do they work & how long have they worked there?
3. Have they got their deposit ready?
4. Will they need a guarantor?
5. How long do they want to rent for?
6. Do they have a partner who might also be staying, either permanently or occasionally at the property?
7. Do they have a car?

You can also ask on the day to see a copy of their references and driving licence so you have some way of tracking them should they default at a later stage and/or disappear without notice.

A word of warning: referencing, referencing, referencing! (See the next chapter)

Who to work with

If your property is for students, you or your letting agent should have a relationship with local universities and/or colleges, as these organisations may have their own portal for students to rent properties through.

Although most people will look for a rental property online, you may still find local newspapers and shops are good places to advertise, so work with these people and speak to them about the different ways you can advertise your property for rent.

And if you're looking for corporate tenants, it's often worth making yourself known to the Human Resources department of large companies, as a good relationship there can result in back-to-back tenancies and very few void periods – plus rent is sometimes paid by the company, meaning a very low risk of non-payment.

••

Hot Tip

NOTE THE CAR: If the prospective tenant arrives for a viewing in a car, take the number plate and details of the car, as this can help you to track them down should they later not pay their rent and leave the property without a valid forwarding address.

Fast & Efficient Credit Checks & Referencing

Basic Credit Checks
Comprehensive with Referencing
Residential & Commercial

–

Fast Priority Checks
Firms & Limited Companies
International with Referencing

–

Tenant Tracing
Immigration Status

CHAPTER 17
TENANT REFERENCING

Never take shortcuts on referencing – it's just not worth the risk!

There are thousands of tenant references carried out every day, but are they being done correctly?

It's crucial to get the referencing process right when selecting a tenant to rent your property. If you take any shortcuts, you're likely at some stage to end up with a rogue tenant who will stay in your property, not pay any rent and cause damage. Too many landlords end up in this situation because they 'thought the tenant seemed OK'!

To give you an idea of how likely it is that a tenant will default on their rent, we're running hundreds of cases at any one time in our office, with clients ranging from inexperienced landlords right through to some of the largest property investors and lettings companies in the UK!

There have been two changes in recent years which affected the referencing process:

General Data Protection Regulations (GDPR)
GDPR came into force on 25th May 2018, and means you have to be extremely careful, and transparent, with the personal information you hold on tenants, guarantors and potential tenants.

GDPR concerns the handling and storage of people's personal information, which includes but is not limited to name and address, email address, car registration number, NI number etc.

The regulations are too complex to explain in detail here but some examples include:

- keeping people's personal information (both physical and digital) secure
- gaining their explicit consent before adding them to mailing lists or, for example, passing their details onto a third party for background checks
- only storing their details for as long as you have their consent or for as long as is necessary
- being able to produce all the information you have about somebody on their request – and delete it if required

Unless you are an expert in data protection, it is important to seek advice on GDPR and how it affects you as a landlord. If you are a member of a landlord association – which is highly recommended – they should be able to help. The Residential Landlords Association (RLA) has a useful guide here: https://news.rla.org.uk/are-you-ready-for-gdpr.

Right to Rent legislation
Another change to the referencing process came with the introduction of Right to Rent legislation in February 2016, which means you have to ensure all your tenants have the right to rent a property in the UK and are not here illegally. These need to be done prior to the signing and moving in of a tenancy agreement.

I was a bit fearful of this new law coming in, putting even more onus on landlords and agents, arguing that they are doing the government immigration office's job for them. I was also concerned that some landlords could discriminate against certain tenants, as they are worried about being fined. Now, the new Home Secretary Sajid Javid is looking at the Right to Rent laws in the wake of the Windrush scandal,

Referencing a tenant isn't difficult, but it does require meticulous attention to detail. Make sure you are not rushed in your referencing process by the tenant; this is part of your lettings process and you are piecing together a jigsaw to ensure the tenant can pay the rent for the full term of the tenancy. If things do not make sense from the tenant's referencing, ask questions. And if tenants are not providing the info listed below, why not?

There is now a database of Rogue Landlords, so isn't it about time we had a national database of Bad Tenants? I've been calling for this for years and it would be really useful for landlords.

There are 10 key checks you need to make before accepting a tenant into your property:

Key steps

1. **Get proof of identity**
   This is either a driver's licence or passport - ideally the driver's licence, as this will have an address on it you can check out. But don't forget these alone won't prove their identity – they can be doctored!

2. **Right to Rent check**
   You and your agent are responsible for checking a tenant has the legal right to be living in the UK and these checks apply to everyone, regardless of whether they are a foreign national or not. All tenants aged 18 and over must be checked, even if they are not named on the tenancy agreement.

   You could be sent to prison for five years or get an unlimited fine for renting a property in England to someone who you knew or had 'reasonable cause to believe' didn't have the right to rent in the UK, or cannot prove you made these checks. Alternatively, you could get a 'referral notice', which could result in a 'civil penalty'.

You will need to obtain at least one document from a set list from the tenant, examples of which include a birth certificate, passport or a valid work permit. UK armed forces personnel are exempt from immigration control under Section 8 of the 1971 Immigration Act; a forces identity card can be accepted in conjunction with other paperwork. The full list of acceptable documents is available on the government website: www.gov.uk/government/publications/right-to-rent-document-checks-a-user-guide.

Make sure you keep a paper trail on correspondence with the prospective tenant, to cover yourself. If you find any issues, you are required to report the tenant to the authorities

For more information on Right to Rent, visit www.gov.uk/check-tenant-right-to-rent-documents

3. Take their National Insurance number
This proves they are working in the UK and gives you an opportunity to know if the work they are doing is legitimate. If it's not, they could be made unemployed at any time.

4. Check their address
If you haven't received proof of their current address already, ask for a utility bill. This is an electric or gas bill, NOT a mobile phone bill.

5. Ask for copies of their last three months' bank statements
These are a great source of information. They help you to understand what the tenant spends their money on, when they get paid, how regularly that payment is and how much 'spare' they have at the end of the month should something go wrong with their wages or other expenditure.

6. **Get an employer's reference**

    It's essential to secure this via both a telephone conversation and a letter on the company's headed paper. It's very easy for tenants to 'doctor' a paper reference and simply give you a friend's mobile number to call. So make sure you check out the company and call them on their main switchboard to ask for the person who has written the reference letter. You can also check out the company with Companies House online to make sure it exists.

7. **Take a reference from their last landlord**

    As young people are now renting for some years prior to buying, they may be moving to your property from another rented home, so ask for a reference from that landlord. Check the landlord that has written the reference is the same person who owns the property by looking on the Land Registry – it costs just £3 for the information. Ring the landlord, ideally on a landline, to confirm your tenant/s did rent the property from them and, if you're still not sure, you could go to their previous property and visit the neighbours to check whether there were any problems. Also ask for a copy of their current or past tenancy agreement at this address. We have come across friends/relatives that will lie and pretend to be the previous landlord.

8. **Reference any guarantors**

    If the tenant uses a guarantor, then you must reference that person as in the same way you would a tenant. For example, if the guarantor is a homeowner, then check they actually own the property via the Land Registry. Also, make sure you ring the guarantor to double-check everything with them, as they may not appreciate the importance of what they have signed.

9. **Make credit reference checks**

    Credit checks are helpful, to show that tenants pay their debts on time and haven't got any county court judgements against them. Normally you would charge the tenant for credit checks to be carried out but the rules on charging tenant fees are changing so this will not be possible in the future. Many lettings agents and landlords rely solely on these to reference a tenant but in my view it's not enough. Only by making all 10 checks I've included here can you be sure you've done all you can.

I would always recommend using a Tenant Referencing company, especially if you are inexperienced at this or strapped for time. Costs can vary from £10-£40. I can recommend these companies:

- www.tenantverify.co.uk
- www.fccparagon.com
- www.landlordreferencing.co.uk

10. **Trust your gut!**
    Regardless of the results of the above checks, if you have any doubts as to whether this is the right person to rent your property, don't go ahead. If you phone them and it always goes to voicemail, they're late getting their deposit to you or it takes a long time to have them referenced, then they will probably cause you hassle at some time during their stay.

Who to work with

Tenant referencing companies: www.tenantverify.co.uk, www.fccparagon.com, www.landlordreferencing.co.uk

Credit check agencies:
www.experian.co.uk, www.equifax.co.uk, www.noddle.co.uk

The Land Registry: www.landregistry.gov.uk

County Court Judgment search: www.registrytrust.co.uk

The Home Office: www.gov.uk/government/organisations/home-office

Facebook, Twitter and other social media: it's always worth checking to see what prospective tenants are sharing online about themselves, as you may discover something very telling.

Questions to ask yourself

1. Have I carried out every one of my 10 tenant checks?
2. Have I verified the information given to me, ie checked official documents haven't been forged?
3. Do I have any doubts about the tenant being credible? (If you do, wait for a better tenant to turn up or it could cost you thousands of pounds in lost rent and property damage!)

● ●

Hot Tip

KNOW THE NEIGHBOURS: The neighbours of your rental property can be very helpful in giving an early warning if you have a bad tenant, so make sure you give them your contact details and show you are approachable, should the tenants cause them a problem.

CHAPTER 18
HOW TO DEAL WITH GUARANTORS

Some tenants may not have the best of records, may come from abroad or – for whatever reason – struggle to find the deposit. This doesn't mean they will be a bad tenant; it just means you need to go the extra step to secure your rental income.

Getting a guarantor to undertake responsibility for the rent is your safety net.

A guarantor is a third party who agrees to pay any rent, should the tenant default, and they are also typically liable for any damage to the property if the tenant can't afford to – or won't – pay for it themselves.

Guarantors are most commonly used for:

- First-time tenants, who may not have a steady income, such as students
- People with a bad credit history
- People on benefits, who have very little spare cash
- Those from abroad who can't be referenced in the UK.

In these cases, trying to obtain a guarantor if possible is a no-brainer; "two heads are better than one" is my motto. Try to make sure the guarantor is a homeowner/business owner and has assets. I've acted for family members in the past as a guarantor, so they can secure a rental, as this was a condition from their landlord.

From a tenancy agreement perspective, the guarantor can simply sign the agreement on behalf of the tenant, provided the agreement explains under what circumstances the guarantor is liable to pay monies to the landlord.

Make sure you have had your guarantor's agreement checked out, as we see all types. Some agreements say the guarantor is liable for just the fixed term of the tenancy and some say the guarantor is liable for the term the tenant resides in the property, until they vacate, making them liable for the rent and any damage or theft of items listed on the inventory.

Typically, it's parents or family that become guarantors, but it may be the tenant's employer, if they're moving on their behalf or, in some cases, the local authority.

Unfortunately, many agents and landlords simply don't take nearly enough care when securing a guarantor, which rather negates the point of getting one in the first place!

If you accept a guarantor, you have to carry out credit checks and reference them in the same way you would a tenant, to make sure they have the means to pay, should you need to claim against them.

It's also essential they sign a formal guarantor agreement, which includes their full name and that of the tenant, the dates of the tenancy, details of the property and how much they're able and willing to guarantee.

The two main issues you have to look out for are:

1. is the guarantor truly who they say they are and not just a friend or acquaintance of the tenant?
2. are they fully aware of what the tenant is asking of them and able to pay up, if required?

Key steps

1. **Agree with the tenant that a guarantor is required**
   Talk to the tenant, explain why you need a guarantor in order for them to rent the property and tell them what they need to explain to the person they're asking.

2. **Take the guarantor's details**
   Ask your tenant to supply the guarantor's address, landline, mobile number and email address.

3. **Explain the agreement to the guarantor yourself**
   Be aware that not all tenants explain the role of the guarantor to the person they are asking to sign the agreement. Some say it's just a 'reference of good character' and don't give them all the paperwork. If possible, get the guarantor to come to the property with the tenant so you can meet them in person. If that's not possible, make sure you speak to them on the phone and send the tenancy agreement to them by recorded delivery. You can also get a guarantor to simply sign a Rent Guarantee Agreement. Make sure you have a contract that includes a guarantor agreement, in or with the tenancy agreement, and have it witnessed by an independent person when the guarantor signs.

4. **Reference check the guarantor**
   You need to treat the guarantor as if they are renting the property themselves and carry out the 10 checks detailed in Chapter 16.

5. **Keep up to date**
   Ensure the agreement is always updated with any new legal rules and regulations.

6. **Renewals**
   If the tenant renews the tenancy agreement, you will need a new signature from the guarantor to confirm their continued protection.

Who to work with

To make sure you have a credible guarantor agreement that will stand up in court, you should work with a legal lettings specialist. Alternatively, you can download guarantor agreements from legal document websites, but make sure you always use the latest version and keep up to date with changes.

Questions to ask the guarantor

1.   Is the guarantor a UK citizen?
2.   Can they meet you at your office or at the property?
3.   Are they aware they have been nominated by the tenant to guarantee their rent and any damages?
4.   Do they know the tenant personally?
5.   What is their relationship to the tenant?
6.   Do they own a home and what is the address?
7.   Who is their employer and what are the details of their employment?
8.   For sharers, do you need a guarantor for each tenant?
9.   Are they acting for one or all tenants?
10. How much are they able and willing to be liable for?

•••

Hot Tip

Make sure during the tenancy that the guarantor's details are up to date, for example, if they move you will need to secure a new forwarding address, so you know where to chase the guarantor if the tenant defaults on their rent.

CHAPTER 19
BEWARE OF PROFESSIONAL BAD TENANTS

'Professional' bad tenants are serial rogues who prey on landlords. It's a huge problem within the industry and I have appeared on a number of TV programmes that have reported on and exposed them, including Tenants from Hell, Meet the Landlords and Inside Out. This media coverage highlights the huge problem and the fact that spotting them is often not easy. They are usually charming, pay the deposit very quickly and will even give you a few months of rent up front to lull you into a false sense of security. Then the problems will start!

Since 1999, we have carried out more than 35,000 instructions against bad tenants and it never ceases to amaze me the types of people that default on rent. I've seen teachers and even barristers rent properties and then not pay anything at all. They know the law and are happy to create sham defences and spurious claims to try and delay any repossession action you might take. They know how to make sure you spend months and thousands of pounds trying to get rid of them and they know just when to leave.

Top 10 traits of professional bad tenants

1. They will target amateur landlords who haven't let before or whose property has been on the market for a little while, as they know they'll be desperate to find a tenant.
2. Any 'official documents' they give you will probably be forged, so you need to check them with the previous landlord, employer or bank to make sure they are genuine.
3. Most professional bad tenants will try to avoid letting agents and landlords who use referencing companies. They may even say to you, "don't worry about referencing, I'll give you a few months' extra

up front" and use the excuse that they want to move in quickly.

4. They will not want to give you photo ID or current employment details. They may say they're self-employed, which adds to your problems if they try to run a business from your premises and rack up a load of bills on the back of it! If they give you a foreign document that you don't recognise as some kind of proof of identity or occupation, ask for something else more recognisable. Remember, you or your agent could be fined if you let a property to someone who turns out to be here illegally. Check out online whether their ID matches the official document via: www.gov.uk/government/news/immigration-bill-becomes-law

5. They will often be keen to give you three or more months' rent. This is a bit of a giveaway that all is not above board – why would they do this if they didn't have to?

6. Bad tenants will also not want to hand over any bank statements. What they often produce is a building society book, which doesn't show their spending habits at all!

7. They probably will make an excuse as to why they can't give you any recent utility bills. Generally speaking, if they're not paying rent, there are other bills they're not paying either!

8. If they're part of a criminal gang that wants to set up a cannabis factory, they may well offer to pay all the rent for their agreement period in advance, in return for 'privacy'. Don't ever accept this deal as you must always be able to inspect your property at any stage.

9. Rogue tenants are not likely to ask any questions about seeing the Energy Performance Certificate, a gas or electrical safety certificate or worry about their deposit being protected. Good tenants *are* likely to ask for these things.

10. Rogue tenants often won't worry about a tenancy agreement either. They'll be happy just for confirmation of tenancy in a letter, so you have no legal framework to fall back on when you realise you need to evict them!

Hot Tip

REFERENCES: If any tenant offers to pay you more rent up front than required, make sure you carry out our top 10 tenant checks (Chapter 16), rather than take the cash. Evicting a tenant can cost tens of thousands of pounds, so avoid this situation in the first place by putting the checks in place.

Case Study

There are 'professional bad tenants', whose mission is to try to trick their way into a property and stay there as long as possible, rent free.

Landlord Action has dealt with more than 35,000 cases in the last 18 years and I'm sure it won't come as any surprise that we have evicted the same tenant twice or more on a few occasions.

If a landlord takes out full referencing or a rent guarantee policy that can normally flush them out, as they will not want to – or will not be able to – provide full references, as their past can catch up with them. So landlords need to be on guard at all times and never be rushed during this process. Dot your i's and cross your t's.

We had a recent case which is featured on Bad Tenants, Rogue Landlords, where the tenant produced a fake screenshot to the landlord showing that one month's rent and deposit had been paid into her account, which was false. Unfortunately the landlord naively did not check her account and gave her the keys. She also did not carry out the full range of references. Yes, you guessed it, she didn't pay any rent while in the property, until we evicted her.

CHAPTER 20
CANNABIS FACTORIES

Having a property turned into a cannabis factory is one of the worst things that can happen to a landlord. As well as the untold damage caused to your property, the police will treat it as a crime scene, so you won't be able to carry out any repairs or relet the property until their investigation is over.

Raids on cannabis factories may have fallen in recent years – according to a BBC report (www.bbc.co.uk/news/uk-33821227), they dropped by more than 17% in 2015 – but this does not mean the problem is going away and may merely indicate that police resources are being directed elsewhere.

Criminal activity on your property is just one part of the problem of cannabis factories. Other issues include:

- electricity meters being doctored and huge bills run up
- holes being made in walls and ceilings for large ventilation pipes
- carpets being torn out and replaced by polythene sheets
- doors and windows being taped over with black polythene
- water damage
- damp, condensation and general problems from lack of any ongoing maintenance
- greater risk of fire due to the deadly combination of heat lamps, overloaded sockets and watering systems – in many cases, the cannabis factory is only discovered when fire breaks out.

All this damage usually costs tens of thousands of pounds to rectify and you may well not be covered by your insurance.

The best way to avoid criminal gangs taking over your property is to carry out all the tenant referencing checks, as per Chapter 16. However, the problem with criminal gangs is that they tend to be very good at getting false names and identities, so will often pass these checks fairly easily.

What they will find more difficult to get around are bank statements and the checks you can make to follow up the information in them. Getting a copy of their driving licence and a photo can be helpful, as well as a recent utility bill. If these all match up well, you should be able to avoid falling foul of this type of criminal activity.

Police can detect cannabis factories through conducting 'flyovers' by helicopters with special heat-sensing surveillance equipment. This picks up any suspiciously large amounts of electrical activity coming from a property and is used in conjunction with traditional surveillance on the ground to see who is coming and going from the property.

Key steps

1. DO NOT accept three to six months' cash rent in advance.
2. DO NOT accept putting the utilities in your name.
3. DO carry out all our 10 referencing steps.
4. Look out for signs of illegal activity. If your property is being used as a cannabis factory, you'll probably notice some of the following:
   o Blacked out windows
   o Night-time visits to the property
   o Lots of short-term visitors throughout the day
   o Birds congregating on the roof in cold weather, or snow on the roof melting unusually quickly
   o Noise from the cooling fans
   o Pungent smells from the property
   o Lots of black bin liners and laundry bags
   o Excessive amounts of compost bags – with no obvious signs of any gardening taking place!
5. DO NOT confront the perpetrators if you're suspicious. Cannabis factories are often guarded and the tenants could be armed. They may also have hard-wired the doors and windows to the electricity, so you'll literally get a shock if you try to get in!

6. DO contact your local police and report your suspicion. Also, make sure you visit crimestoppers-uk.org to see the latest signs to look out for.
7. Make sure you form a good relationship with the neighbours of your buy to let property. They can be your eyes and ears and give you all sorts of useful information about what's going on.

• •

Hot Tip

GET THE RIGHT INSURANCE: To help protect yourself from criminal gangs who may cause a lot of damage to your property, make sure malicious damage insurance is included in your policy. Recommended: www.totallandlordinsurance.co.uk.

CHAPTER 21
TYPES OF TENANCY AGREEMENTS

Getting the right type of tenancy agreement in place to protect you and your property is vital. Without an up-to-date, accurate and legal tenancy agreement, in writing, it can make life much more difficult for a landlord.

We often have to go to court to gain possession when there is only an oral tenancy agreement.

Before you actually rent a property out, especially if it was once your own home (primary residence), make sure you have written permission from your lender. If you don't, the mortgage agreement you have in place may make it illegal for you to let the property altogether, or under certain terms.

If you have a leasehold property, make sure you also check the lease, as some prohibit letting or allow it but specify the kind of tenancy agreement you need to have.

There are four main tenancy agreements:

Assured Shorthold Tenancy agreement
An Assured Shorthold Tenancy (AST) is the most popular tenancy agreement. It sets out the terms and conditions of letting the property for both you and the tenant. An AST can be periodic from the start although the general approach is that the tenancy lasts for a minimum of six months as that is the soonest you can obtain possession of the property under a Section 21 notice. The benefit to you of using an AST is that after the end of the fixed term you have the right to take your property back.

If you have a mortgage, the lender is likely to have stipulated in their terms and conditions that you rent your property out on this basis.

An AST sets out:

1. Contact details for the tenant and landlord
2. The rent agreed and the date it will be paid
3. The time frame the property will be rented for
4. The rights and responsibilities of the landlord
5. The rights and responsibilities of the tenant
6. What happens on termination

Within 30 days of receiving a deposit on an AST it is a legal requirement to give the tenant – and anyone who has contributed to the deposit – the following prescribed information:

- Information about your chosen deposit protection scheme, including the official scheme leaflet
- A copy of the deposit protection certificate/receipt
- Gas safety certificate – this should be provided before the tenant moves in (see Chapter 10)
- Energy Performance Certificate
- A paper copy of, or link to, the government's How to Rent guide, which can be found here: www.gov.uk/government/publications/how-to-rent. Make sure you have an up-to-date copy as it is revised frequently.

The serving of the prescribed information is as important as protecting the deposit. If the deposit is not protected and/or the prescribed information is not provided to the tenant within 30 days then you cannot serve a Section 21 notice and could be liable to a claim for up to three times the deposit amount.

The government's How to Rent guide is also a useful source of information about renting and letting, especially regarding both your and the tenant's rights and responsibilities: gov.uk/government/publications/how-to-rent

It is one in a series of 'How to' guides from the government, which now includes How to Let, How to Lease and How to Rent a Safe Home. You can find them all here: www.gov.uk/government/collections/housing-how-to-guides.

House/flat share agreements

Typically, if you have sharers in a property, an AST is used, but in joint tenant names. Additional clauses are needed to state that:

1. The sharers are jointly and severally liable for payment of the whole rental amount.
2. Any damage to the property is paid for equally by all tenants, whether they were responsible or not.

This is quite an undertaking, especially if the tenants don't know each other. It tends to work with groups of tenants all taking the property at the same time – such as several work colleagues or a group of students – but where the tenants don't know each other, it may be better to give each their own agreement. That way, if one of them is causing problems or not paying rent, you can let the problem tenant go and keep the good ones.

Excluded Tenancy or Renting a Room

You usually rent a room 'under a licence'. The agreement will be similar to an AST, except there will be stipulations as to what is private to the tenant (for example, their bedroom), what parts of the property are private to the landlord, and what parts are communal. This is usual when the landlord is resident and sharing the property with the tenant.

As you will typically share kitchen and bathroom facilities and bills, the licence agreement will set out which facilities are shared, how they should be kept and what contribution the tenant should make to the bills. Utility bills are usually included, but any personal phone calls are paid separately by the tenant.

Finally, although the rules on evicting the tenant are much lighter for the landlord, you still have to apply to the court and secure their permission for any eviction.

Assured Agreements

Before the AST was introduced, the usual form of contract was an Assured Agreement, which gave many more rights to the tenant. This agreement only exists today if the property has been rented to the same tenants since before 28th February 1997. With Assured Agreements:

1. There is no limit to the length of time the tenants can rent the property.
2. Tenants have a right to go to a 'fair rent review' if they feel any rental increases are unfair.
3. The agreement can be extended to include a spouse, partner or, in some cases, their children too.

Private Residential Tenancy – Scotland

Big changes have taken place in Scotland recently. Private Residential Tenancies were introduced on 1st December 2017 which mean landlords have to offer open-ended tenancies, give longer notice periods and rent increases are limited to one per year. Break clauses and fixed term tenancies are no longer allowed. There is more information about the Scotland changes in Chapter 5 and online at www.rentingscotland.org.

Key steps

1. **Creating Tenancy Agreements yourself**

   You can buy a tenancy agreement 'off the shelf' – online or from stationers – but although it may seem like you're saving legal fees by doing it yourself, be aware that one error or omission in the tenancy agreement may make it invalid, so you do need to know what you're doing and keep it up to date.

2. **Having bespoke agreements drawn up by a lawyer**

Not all legal companies or solicitors are renting and letting experts. Make sure if you do secure a bespoke letting agreement, you use someone who is experienced in this sector. Many letting agents have their own agreement, which will save you a lot of hassle. We offer them at www.landlordaction.co.uk.

From my perspective, having a fuller contract with more detailed clauses tends to help you down the line, when disputes arise. We often sell such tenancy agreements to landlords.

3. **Ending the Tenancy Agreement**

Make sure you're clear on what notices need to be issued and when, in order for you to legally retake possession of the property at the end of the tenancy agreement. Under an AST you are required to serve a Notice called a Section 21, giving the tenant two months to vacate the property. (See Chapter 43).

4. **Dealing with breach of tenancy**

When a tenant is in breach of their agreement, it's especially important to ensure you issue the correct notices, at the right time and in the right order, and you should take legal advice on this, as mistakes can void any paperwork and delay the process of evicting the tenant. See Part 3 for detailed information on breaches and evictions.

If a tenant simply decides that they want to leave a property before the end of the fixed term, they would typically be liable for any outstanding rent payments until the end of the agreement.

For example, if they've signed an AST for six months and want to leave after four months, they are liable for the final two months' rent.

In reality, I think it's better to help the tenant move on, if that's what they want or need to do, especially if it's due to difficult circumstances (family problems or loss of job). What you can do is try to find a new tenant and just charge the existing tenant the costs you incur to find someone new. This is a more practical way of dealing with such a scenario, rather than leaving a property vacant for months until the end of the tenancy and having to try to trace the tenant to a new forwarding address and pursue them through the courts.

It's important to keep up to date with what's happening legally with tenancy agreements. All the political parties seem to be keen to make tenancies longer but no action has been taken. Currently if you want to let your property long term, you can, but make sure you don't fall foul of your contract with the mortgage company, who might restrict tenancies to six months and can still evict for non-payment of rent.

Note: At the time of writing this book, the government has just closed a consultation on three-year tenancy agreements with a six-month break clause, with a view to offering tenants greater security. I have filed a response to this consultation on behalf of Landlord Action.

. . . .

Hot Tip

KNOW YOUR TENANT TYPE. Do your research as to what type of tenant you have and what category they fall into, so you give the correct agreement.

CHAPTER 22
ESSENTIAL TENANCY AGREEMENT CLAUSES

When it comes to tenancy agreements, you name it, we have seen it at Landlord Action; they can be 40 pages long, or two sides, or hand written on a piece of A4 paper.

As it currently stands, tenancy agreements can be either verbal or written, but it's by far the best practice to put your agreement in writing so there's a clear record of rights and responsibilities and of exactly what was agreed between you and the tenant. If you need to go to court, a verbal agreement is very hard to argue.

It's so important the agreement is written in plain English and that whatever agreement you use is kept up to date and includes certain clauses to protect you, as a landlord. Our solicitors in our office often draft up bespoke specialist agreements for landlords and letting agents, such as commercial rent to rent, renewal/addendum, guarantee agreements, student lettings, company tenancies etc.

Making sure you have the correct agreement is so important; is it a room let, room share or the whole house? Are you renting to a business, like a limited company, so a company agreement is needed? Have you agreed there should be a guarantor? If so, a guarantor agreement is needed (see Chapter 17).

The key thing to be aware of is that you can't simply invent your own rules and regulations – tenancy agreements have to abide by statutory law, as set out by the Housing Act. Any clause that suggests either party has fewer rights than those given by common law or statute is not valid and will not be enforceable by law.

Further measures to protect tenants were introduced in the Deregulation Act 2015, which mean you must:

- Provide the tenant with prescribed information, including a copy of a valid EPC, gas safety certificate and the latest government's version of the How to Rent Guide. The full list is detailed in Chapter 10.
- Protect the tenant's deposit in an approved scheme (see Chapter 25)

In addition, the Act places restrictions on serving Section 21 notices; this is explained in full in Chapter 43.

To make sure your agreement is valid and protects you as much as possible, you must include the following clauses:

1. Your address and details, without which you can't secure rent or serve any notices on the tenant in England and Wales.

2. The date of the agreement, which should be the same as the tenancy start date. This is so that you can tie in the amount of rent paid to the date of the tenancy.

3. Address of the property and details of any additional space that the tenant is renting, such as a garage or parking. If you don't detail all the space, it may be difficult to prove in court that it was included in the rental agreement.

4. The names of all tenants renting the property, making sure you amend the tenancy agreement if the existing tenant moves someone else in. If you don't include everyone on the tenancy agreement, they may be more difficult to evict if problems occur.

5. The length of the tenancy agreement, so that the courts know when you can claim for possession. The government is currently reviewing plans to reduce barriers for landlords to offer longer tenancies.

6. Details of the rent, including how much is to be paid, the date on which it's due and penalties for late or non-payment, be they financial or eviction. If you don't specify when arrears can be claimed and acted upon, it's more difficult to take legal action against the tenant.

7. The responsibilities of both parties. It must be clear what the tenant is responsible for and what you need to do. Confusion can easily arise over who keeps the garden tidy, who cleans the windows, what happens if an appliance stops working and whether the property has to be professionally cleaned at the end of the tenancy.

8. Details of the process to increase the rent, which must be clearly explained to the tenant so that it's fair and they can't legitimately oppose any increases or threaten to report you to rent control.

9. Details of any deposit taken, detailing that you are compliant with one of the government-approved protection schemes. If you don't protect the deposit and correctly inform your tenant, you could fail to regain possession of your property.

10. Break clause. In England and Wales, if you're giving the tenant a 12-month tenancy, it's advisable to have a six-month break clause.

It's important to make sure your tenant signs the tenancy agreement, witnessed, and returns it to you before they move in. We have seen many cases where the tenant has refused to return the tenancy agreement, but is in possession of the property and we have possible future problems at court.

Key steps

Making sure you have the right tenancy clauses in place is an on-going job, as the rules change. To ensure you are always protected:

1. **Be clear on responsibilities**
   Make sure your tenants understand what you're responsible for looking after and what they need to do, both in terms of the property and the paperwork, including rent. This will help avoid problems from the start and reduce the likelihood of the tenants breaking their agreement.

2. **Put everything in writing**
   If the tenant does break the agreement, make sure you notify them in writing of what they've done, what they need to do to put it right and what action you will have to take if they don't.

3. **Keep in touch with legal changes**
   You could simply keep checking online, but the best ways to make sure your tenancy agreement is always up to date are by working closely with a legal company or joining a local landlord accreditation scheme who will automatically advise you when updates are required.

Who to work with

It's up to you how you keep up to date with your legals, but I'd recommend you use an expert lettings legal company. Many of the landlords I work on behalf of don't have a good tenancy agreement in place, which limits what I can do when things go badly wrong.

A good lettings legal company will make sure your tenancy agreement is always up to date and, importantly, that it doesn't include any clauses that are opposed to the statute law or are considered by law as 'unfair'.

If you use an online legal company, make sure they always send you the most up-to-date version of the agreement.

Questions to ask a lettings legal expert

1. How does the company keep up to date with current legals?
2. How will the company keep you updated of any law changes?
3. Do changes to the law mean the tenant needs to re-sign the agreement?
4. What cover does the company give you if, for any reason, the legal agreement doesn't stand up in court?
5. What happens to that cover if the company goes bust?

••

Hot Tip

ENSURE ALL CLAUSES ARE VALID. Make sure your tenancy agreement includes all the main clauses to protect you and that none of the clauses in the agreement contradict statute.

CHAPTER 23
TENANCY CLAUSES TO AVOID

Unfortunately, too many landlords use tenancy agreements they've either bought 'off the shelf' some time ago or simply copied from a previous rental contract of their own. Two things then tend to follow: the agreement doesn't get updated when there's a change in law and clauses get randomly added or adapted over time.

Just because a tenant signs an agreement, it doesn't mean all the clauses you've put in or amended are legally binding. From a legal perspective, many of the rights and responsibilities of tenants and landlords are not decided by the tenancy agreement – they're set out in the Housing Act 1988. In law, what is set out in statute overrides anything in an agreement between two or more parties.

So many clauses have been introduced into tenancy agreements by landlords, letting agents and even some legal companies, that the Office of Fair Trading has produced reports specifically addressing unfair terms.

Unfair terms and clauses

Clauses in tenancy agreements that are considered 'unfair terms' aren't enforceable. A court will decide whether clauses are fair or unfair. A clause is typically considered unfair when it is weighed far more in favour of one party than another. This is especially the case if the clause takes advantage of the lack of experience of the tenant.

As well as containing fair terms and conditions, the tenancy agreement must also be in plain English and the tenant should be given time to read it themselves and (ideally) have it checked out by their own legal company.

Examples of unfair clauses

Any clause that unfairly limits or excludes your liability – especially if it claims that you're exempt from any liability for actions of third-party tradesmen or acts that would be considered negligence on your behalf –are highly likely to be deemed unfair, particularly if they exclude liability for injury or death.

Other examples of unfair clauses:

1. Transferring your obligations set out in statute to the tenant, eg making it the tenant's responsibility to carry out gas safety checks.
2. Requiring the tenant carry out repairs and maintenance themselves.
3. Not paying for damage to tenant's property when you're at fault.
4. Requiring the tenant to pay for call-out charges to fix things you're responsible for maintaining.
5. Refusing to carry out works if the tenant doesn't advise you early enough to fix a property problem.
6. Giving yourself the right to enter the property without reasonable notice.
7. Asking the tenant for a deposit without any chance of a refund.
8. Imposing a disproportionately large fine for late rent payment.
9. Any term suggesting that the tenant could be evicted at any time.
10. Any clauses suggesting you can change the agreement without any discussion with the tenant.

Key steps

There are really only two:

1. **Use an up-to-date tenancy agreement**
   Make sure, at the start of each tenancy, that the agreement you're using has been updated with the latest legislation.

2. **Comply with tenancy deposit protection terms and conditions**
The agreement must also adhere to the latest terms and conditions laid out by your chosen tenancy deposit protection scheme.

Who to work with

Ideally, work with a legal company that specialises in lettings. If you buy an off-the-shelf agreement, make sure it's the latest version and don't try to adapt it. You could join a landlord association, which gives you access to free agreements.

If you use a letting agent, they should manage the tenancy agreement for you and accept legal liability for it.

Questions to ask

Before you sign a tenancy agreement, secure answers to the following, in writing, from the company/agent that's supplying it:

1. When was the agreement last updated?
2. Does it contain any clauses that could be considered unfair?
3. Will this agreement stand up in court should the tenant fall into arrears?
4. Does the agreement comply with the court's requirement if you need to evict the tenant?
5. What protection does the agreement give you if the tenant causes damage to your property?
6. What liability do you have within the agreement?
7. Has the tenant been given enough time to read and check the agreement for themselves?

Hot Tip

ALWAYS HAVE A BREAK CLAUSE. If you have to serve a notice for breach of tenancy for 'non rent arrears' (Section 8), weigh up the odds as to whether you think you have a strong enough case to be successful in court – remember it's up to the judge's discretion. You will need to supply strong written evidence to the court, proving the tenant has breached their agreement, and a judge may regard the grounds as too weak – that's why I'd suggest it's always better to serve a Section 21 notice to end the contract. And if you have issued a 12-month agreement, you may have many months to wait before you can get the tenant out; that's why it's so important to have a six-month break clause in England and Wales.

NB: Scottish rules are different and break clauses are no longer permitted. See Chapter 21.

CHAPTER 24
CHARGING DEPOSITS – OR NOT!

Always take a deposit and protect it in a deposit scheme

Many landlords believe it's okay to let a property to a tenant and not take a deposit – and it may be, in certain circumstances. What is definitely not okay is to then take two months' rent 'in lieu' of a deposit, just to try to get around the legislation governing them!

You have to be very clear about whether or not to take a deposit. If you prefer to take a deposit and the tenant is on an Assured Shorthold Tenancy agreement, then you *must* protect it through one of the government-approved tenancy deposit protection schemes (see the next chapter).

If you don't protect the deposit taken under an AST, you'll find it difficult to evict the tenant through the courts and you could end up having to give the whole deposit back, regardless of whether you feel you have good reasons for retaining some. Worse still, you could be ordered by the court to pay three times the deposit amount to the tenant as a penalty.

There's no law that says you have to take a deposit, regardless of whether you're letting rooms in an HMO or a whole house to a family.

There is, in fact, an alternative to the traditional deposit system. New to the market are 'no-deposit insurance' products, which give tenants the opportunity to rent a property without having to put down a hefty deposit. This can be helpful if they struggle to find a large sum of money or are waiting for their deposit from their last property to be returned.

Instead, they typically pay a week's rent up front, and the landlord or letting agent takes out an insurance policy in lieu of the deposit. In the event of a claim, the insurance company reimburses the landlord and chases the tenant for any money owed. We haven't yet seen how this works out in reality as it is still very early days for such schemes.

But if the tenant is struggling to pay a deposit, can they afford the rent? I also believe that some tenants will not realise that, under the terms of the policy, they are liable if the insurance company chases for outstanding monies due to damages at the property.

In my opinion, there is no substitute for having the deposit money safely stored in your account (if using an insurance-backed scheme) or with a third party (if using a custodial scheme).

The deposit is there to give you a financial safety net in case the tenant causes damage to your property, steals or loses any of your possessions, or refuses to pay up. In the worst case scenario, a bad tenant may think that if you're daft enough not to take a deposit, you're not a very diligent landlord (and they'd be right!) so they may pay rent late or not at all and try to stay in the property, rent free, until you evict them.

So, assuming you are going to take a deposit, it should be equivalent to no more than two months' rent – typically four to six weeks' rent, but the government is indicating that in the future this will be capped at six week's rent.

Key steps

1. **Do you need to protect the deposit?**
    Check what deposit rules and regulations apply to your tenancy agreement. If it's an AST, you must protect any money you take in one of the government-approved tenancy deposit protection providers and give the prescribed information about the scheme to the tenant in order to be compliant.

2. **Choose a scheme**
   If you have an AST, you need to decide whether to go with a custodial or insurance-based scheme (see next chapter).

3. **Inform the tenant**
   Once you've protected the deposit, you need to make sure the tenant is aware and they have all the details your chosen scheme makes available for tenants.

4. **Return the deposit**
   At the end of the tenancy agreement, make sure you abide by the rules for returning the deposit to the tenant in the manner set out by the deposit scheme. If the deposit didn't require protection in a scheme, you should return it, less any agreed deductions, within two to three weeks of the tenant leaving the property.

Who to work with

If you have an AST, it's a case of researching the different tenancy deposit protection providers, and choosing the right one for you. If you don't have to protect the deposit, it is good practice to keep any monies taken in a separate bank account but don't make the mistake of dipping into this money. If you end up going to court for any reason to do with the tenancy, you want to be able to show that everything is above board.

Questions to ask

In my opinion, there is no question to ask: you should always take a deposit.

Hot Tip

BE CLEAR. Don't confuse 'rent in advance' with the tenant paying a deposit, or it could cause you problems if you have to go to court.

Case Study

Believe it or not, our Landlord Action legal advice line receives calls on a daily basis from landlords wanting to gain possession under Section 21 who have still not protected the tenant's deposit in a deposit scheme or who have protected it late.

If you are in this position, you must return the deposit to the tenant, ideally by BACS transfer to the tenant's account (if you have their bank details). If the tenant is in arrears, they must agree to offset the deposit by consent, with a signature. If you return the cash deposit to the tenant, take a picture or get a signature (some tenants may avoid this). If you have to return a cheque, get picture proof of delivery of this to the property, as this will be needed as evidence if you have to go to court. This must be done before you can serve a Section 21 notice. The evidence of the deposit return is vital, to produce to the court if necessary.

Taking a deposit from a tenant is a must, as is protecting it in the right legal way; it shows commitment to the tenancy and of course offers you some protection against damage...

Fast, simple online protection

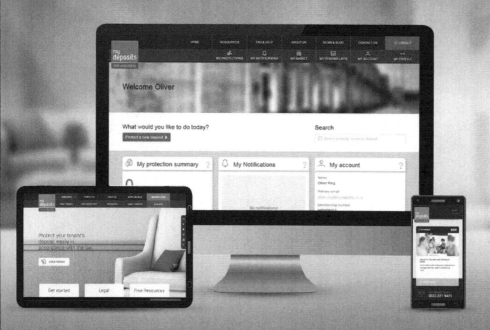

Protect and securely manage your deposits on any device with mydeposits

www.mydeposits.co.uk

CHAPTER 25
CHOOSING A DEPOSIT SCHEME

The average deposit across the country was £1,091 and there are more than 3.76million deposits protected in all the three government schemes, with a combined value of £4.1billion.

In April 2007, tenancy deposit protection schemes were introduced in England and Wales, following complaints by consumer groups that tenants were being cheated out of their deposit money by landlords. They have since been introduced in Scotland (July 2012), Northern Ireland (April 2013) and Jersey (September 2015) – only mydeposits operates across all the regions.

If you rent to a tenant under an Assured Shorthold Tenancy agreement (AST), you need, by law, to protect the tenant's deposit within 30 calendar days of receiving it. You must also supply the tenant with copies of all legal documents and information relating to your chosen scheme within those 30 days.

If your tenant is supported by the local authority, the deposit might be paid over a period of time through their rent, or it may be paid as a loan to you on behalf of the tenant. In this scenario, check with the local authority how to stay on the right side of the law.

There are two different types of scheme:

Custodial – this is where you give the deposit to the tenancy deposit scheme for **'safe keeping'.** When the tenant is due their deposit back, you both authorise the scheme to repay the full deposit, or an agreed amount, to the tenant. If there is any disagreement about deductions, the scheme's dispute resolution service – or, if the parties don't want to use that, the courts – will decide on the amount to be returned to the tenant.

Custodial schemes are free to join and use and are funded through investing the money they hold to secure a return.

Insurance-based – this is where you keep hold of the deposit. You protect it via a scheme that effectively insures the tenant against you not repaying them the correct amount at the end of the tenancy. The insurance-based schemes also provide a free dispute resolution service.

There are three different, government-approved tenancy deposit scheme providers, all of which offer insurance and custodial schemes:

- mydeposits
- Deposit Protection Scheme
- Tenancy Deposit Scheme

Some of these companies offer their schemes through other organisations, for example, mydeposits is owned by the National Landlords Association and Hamilton Fraser Insurance Solutions, who have been part of the private rented sector since 1996.

Key steps

1. **Do you want to manage the deposit yourself?**
    While your first instinct might be to hold on to the money, really consider whether you want the responsibility of keeping and managing deposits.

2. **Compare scheme costs**
    Look at the impact of the cost of keeping and insuring your tenants' deposits, and compare it to handing them over to a custodial scheme.

3. **Research the administration process**
   See how easy it is to use each of the online schemes and check whether there is any additional administration required if the tenancy agreement is renewed or extended. Additional administration and fees are usually only applied if a new AST is issued.

4. **What happens with multiple deposits?**
   If you have multiple properties or one property with multiple tenants, find out what the procedure is for protecting all those deposits.

5. **What if a tenant moves?**
   Check the process for switching a tenant's deposit from one property to another, if the tenant moves.

6. **Return of the deposit**
   Compare how long it will take each scheme to organise repaying the deposit to the tenant – and to you, if your tenant disappears without authorising the amount and you have to instigate a single claim.

7. **How are disputes resolved?**
   Find out how efficient and fair their dispute resolution service is.

8. **Consider the support given**
   See which scheme gives you the best guidance and advice.

Which scheme to choose

To operate a tenancy deposit scheme, a company has to be licensed by the Government. All schemes give advice, but you may find some better than others – look at the scheme's different social media accounts and website resources section to get an idea of the support offered.

If your cash flow is tight, it might be better to use one of the free custodial schemes so you aren't tempted to dip into the deposit and you don't have to pay to insure it. On the other hand, if you're confident you can manage the money well, using an insurance-based scheme enables you to access the money, meaning both the tenant and you can get what you're due more quickly than with a custodial scheme.

If you're letting through an agent, they're likely to have a recommended scheme and any costs may be included in their service and fees. Legal information about the scheme must be provided to the tenant, so using the same one as your letting agent can save you a lot of time and effort.

If you don't use an agent but do belong to a landlord association, you might find they offer their members a better deal with a scheme than you could get by going direct – for example, as the National Landlords Association part-owns mydeposits, you receive a discount with them if you are a member of the NLA.

Questions to ask a scheme provider

1. How much does it cost to use the scheme?
2. How does their administration work?
3. How quickly do they return the deposit to the tenant?
4. How does their single claims process work and how quickly will you get the deposit back?
5. What percentage of disputes are settled in the landlord's favour?

Hot Tip

CONSIDER RECOMMENDED SCHEMES. You can usually save money and get a better level of support by choosing a scheme that's offered by your landlord association or using your letting agent's chosen scheme.

Case Study

mydeposits reported on a dispute where the landlord was claiming £525 for redecoration due to mould.

Evidence submitted included an independent inventory which showed mould staining, patchy paintwork, scuff marks and cracked plaster at the start of the tenancy.

An independent check-out report showed further mould and mildew stains, so the landlord was claiming for redecoration due to mould.

The Adjudicator agreed that the mould and damp problem had grown during the tenancy but an independent damp specialist report showed that this was due to structural issues with the property rather than the tenant's actions. This – and the evidence of mould staining at the start of the tenancy – meant the tenant was not held liable for redecorating costs.

CHAPTER 26
KEEPING YOUR PROPERTY IN GOOD CONDITION

The English Housing Survey 2015-16 tells us that 28% of properties in the private rental sector are considered 'non-decent', which is a drop from 33% in 2012-13, but still represents the highest of any tenure.

According to the rest of the survey, rental properties represent some of our oldest property stock, with 34% having been built before 1919 – nearly 100 years ago! So it's no surprise that damp is one of the biggest problems properties – and therefore tenants – suffer.

One of the biggest issues I see is the lack of money landlords put aside for maintaining and upgrading their property. It's not enough to allocate funds for new carpets, curtains and the odd paint job; you need to properly budget and plan for major works, such as roof repairs, damp proofing, rewiring and upgrading kitchens, bathrooms and boilers, the cost of which can run into tens of thousands of pounds over the lifetime of your buy-to-let investment.

If you don't keep up to date with maintenance and upgrades, your property's condition will suffer and you'll end up with poor tenants who don't look after it, making things worse. A poor quality property will be worth a lot less than one in good condition, which not only affects the amount of rent you can charge, but also might negatively impact the capital value and therefore your ability to remortgage.

You also need to make sure your property meets the minimum energy efficiency standard (MEES), which means, since 1st April 2018, you can no longer start or renew a tenancy on a property with an EPC of F or G. There is more about this in Chapter 10.

As far as I'm concerned, keeping your property well maintained is essential in order to succeed as a landlord. I've seen the kind of damage bad tenants can inflict on a property and know how important it is to make sure you provide quality accommodation that attracts tenants who care about living in a decent home and will look after it for you.

Key steps

1. **Create a plan and budget**
   A surveyor can advise on what works are likely to be necessary over the lifetime of a property, or you can simply use your common sense. Think about when works to the fabric of the property might be required (roof, wiring, repointing, etc), when fixtures and fittings will need updating or replacing (kitchen, bathroom) and how often the property will need repainting, new carpets, etc. You should then be able to put together monthly, annual, 3-5 year, 10, 15 and 20-year costs and budget accordingly.

2. **Put together a maintenance checklist**
   Every property will have its weaknesses, such as a leaky roof, poor mortar joints or damp, which should be completely fixed or at least checked regularly and maintained. You should have a checklist for each of your properties, like the one below, detailing every area that could be a potential problem.

   Always work 'top down':

   - Check the roof to see if any tiles are missing
   - Are the chimneys intact or are they blackened, and do they require new flashing on the joints?

- Check the guttering and drains to make sure they aren't leaking and causing damp in the property
- Look above the windows to see whether there are any cracks in the brickwork above – that may suggest lintels are damaged or missing
- Check door and window seams for leaks and broken seals
- Make sure the sanitaryware and radiators aren't leaking
- Make sure kitchen and bathroom seals aren't cracked or mouldy
- Check on the property's energy efficiency by reading the EPC, ideally making sure it reaches the average D rating and at least E.
- You can also find checklists online, from sites such as Propertychecklists.co.uk or english-heritage.org.uk.

3. **Carry the checks out regularly**
   Diarise to carry out a full maintenance check every three to six months and make sure you also check for major issues after bad weather, such as storms, snow or heavy rain.

Who to work with

You can organise for a surveyor to carry out a Condition Report on your property. They need to be qualified either via the Royal Institute of Chartered Surveyors (rics.org/uk) or the Residential Property Surveyors Association (rpsa.org.uk).

Both of these organisations produce a 'condition report', which costs from £250 for standard-sized properties. If you have a portfolio, it would be worth trying to negotiate a day rate to reduce the costs.

Questions to ask

Before you engage them, it's worth asking the surveyor some questions, to make sure they're the best person for the job:

1. Do they own any buy-to-let properties?
2. Do they have an understanding of how to let a property legally?
3. Do they know how to assess the Healthy Home Rating System (HHRS) in your local authority?
4. Do they have professional indemnity insurance?
5. What happens if you have to claim because they have made a mistake?

It is important they don't just do a 'tick box' job on your property. Make sure they're prepared to do a thorough inspection and give you practical advice on how to keep your property well maintained and fix any problems.

Hot Tip

STAY ON TOP OF THINGS. Fix problems quickly so they don't turn into bigger issues. A great property that's regularly maintained and kept in good condition will let quickly, command the best rent and, most importantly, give you the choice of the best tenants.

Case Study

Your buy to let property is your asset. Take your responsibility of being a landlord seriously; the better your property's condition, the easier it will be to rent and this will hopefully limit void periods.

You can imagine I have been in some horror properties, but that's when things go wrong at the end of a tenancy, generally when a landlord is not given access and tenants are not paying the rent.

I know a landlord, who told me on average his turnaround time to relet a property after cleaning, re-decorating etc is about seven days. His comments were: "Voids can seriously hurt you, so I'm on it from when I get the keys back from the outgoing tenants, to have my contractors in on time, to lining up my agents marketing it for new tenants coming in."

CHAPTER 27
TOP 5 ERRORS LANDLORDS MAKE WHEN CHECKING IN A TENANT

The check-in stage is vital in a tenancy; once you've found your tenant, there is more compliance than ever before for landlords to adhere to. If you're unsure or are new to the industry, I always recommend using a letting agent.

Successful tenancies begin with a successful check-in and so this process should not be rushed. Far too often, I see landlords so desperate to get a paying tenant into their property that they cut corners and end up losing far more in time and money than they would have through leaving the property vacant for a little while longer and taking the care to be thorough.

In my experience, these are the six main errors landlords make at the check-in stage:

1. Not collecting a tenancy deposit prior to check-in
Landlords are still failing to protect the deposits in a government-backed scheme within the 30-day period. If you allow the tenant to move into your property without taking a deposit and a month's rent in advance, you leave yourself wide open to never receiving anything from the tenant.

And if you start the tenancy that way, the tenant can stay in the property for up to six months before I'd be able to help you evict them! Remember, if you're planning to use an Assured Shorthold Tenancy agreement, then legally you have to protect any deposit monies via a tenancy deposit scheme (see Chapter 25).

2. Having an inadequate tenancy agreement

There's a lot of paperwork involved in letting and renting a property and it's essential that you get it right so that you're protected if anything goes wrong.

You should have a robust, up-to-date tenancy agreement, with all the relevant information about the tenancy in it, signed and dated by each tenant and by you. If there is any guarantor, they should sign either the agreement with the relevant guarantor clauses added, or a separate deed of guarantee.

At the start of any action against a tenant in arrears, we need to get as much up-to-date paperwork from you as possible, to prove you have let the property legally in the first place. In my business, if we don't get the paperwork 100% right, it makes it so much harder to obtain an order from a judge.

3. Allowing the tenant to let themselves in

If you're busy and the tenants seem to be 'good people', you might be tempted to simply give them the keys and allow them to let themselves into the property. You absolutely cannot do this.

If you don't let the tenant in, go through the inventory and take time to show them around the property, you have no way of proving the condition of the property when they took it over or what items were in the property.

How will they know what to do if the boiler breaks down or where the stopcock is in case of a leak? If you haven't shown them how to properly secure the doors and windows, it could leave your property open to burglary and theft – and more damage.

Always, *always* take time to accompany the check-in!

4. Not carrying out an inventory

An inventory is an essential part of the check-in process - without it you can't prove to a tenancy deposit company or a court that the tenants are responsible for any damage to, or theft from the property.

Allowing the tenant to check in without an inventory is essentially handing them a free pass to treat the property however they like and you won't be able to pursue them for compensation for any losses.

See the next chapter for more information on inventories.

5. Not providing instructions for appliances
Appliances can be dangerous things. I've seen them flood properties, start fires and cause a huge amount of damage. Something as simple as not leaving instructions for a cooker, boiler, waste disposal unit or washing machine could cost you – and the tenant – dearly.

Better than just leaving instruction manuals, help your tenant to understand how everything works. If they're distracted when you check them in, offer to pop back a few days after they have moved everything in, to explain how to operate and maintain the systems and appliances, and let them know who to call if they have any problems.

6. Failing to comply with the Deregulation Act (came in 1st October 2015)
A landlord must provide a tenant with a valid EPC (Energy Performance Certificate), gas safety certificate, valid proof that smoke and carbon monoxide alarms are working, along with a How to Rent Guide, prior to the tenant moving into the property. These must all be acknowledged and signed for by the tenant

If this prescribed information is not provided, the landlord is unable to serve a section 21 notice at a later date and it becomes harder to gain access in some instances, once the tenant is in the property.

Key steps

1. **Agree when the check-in will take place**
   Find a mutually convenient date and time to check the tenant in – Friday or Saturday is usually most convenient for working tenants,

so you may have to be flexible. Make sure the tenant is aware the check-in process could take several hours.

2. Go through the paperwork
If you haven't already, go through the tenancy agreement with the tenant, highlighting their responsibilities and ensuring they understand the terms of the tenancy agreements. Make sure you have served the valid deregulation documents before the tenant moves into the property; being a valid EPC, gas safety certificate and the latest How to Rent Guide with proof of working smoke and carbon monoxide alarms. This must be done.

3. Go through the inventory
Walk around the property with the tenant, checking the condition of every room; what contents you've supplied and the condition; the exterior of the property and any gardens and outbuildings, against the inventory.

4. Show the tenant how everything works
Make sure they know where the stopcock and fuse box are, how the heating system works, how to safely use all the appliances, etc.

5. Confirm contact details
Make sure the tenant has the details of whoever is managing the let (you or an agent) and also of who to contact in case of emergencies, particularly during out-of-office hours and on holidays. You should also double check the details you hold for the tenant, making sure you have a mobile number and an email address, and try to obtain details of a next of kin.

6. Check they know what to do in the event of a fire, flood, burglary or other damage

7. **Go through security measures**

   Explain how to keep the property safe via door and window locks, highlighting what the tenants need to do to ensure your insurance remains valid.

Who to work with

It can take a few hours to carry out a proper check-in and you want the property let as soon as possible, so if you're going to be rushed or are unable to do it yourself when the tenants want to move in – perhaps because you work full time – then it may be better to outsource the check-in to a local letting agent or inventory clerk.

Since 2014 all agents have had to belong to a redress scheme, which deals with escalated complaints. Recently, one of the redress schemes, Ombudsman Services, announced it was withdrawing from complaints handling in the property sector from August 2018, leaving just two: the Property Ombudsman and the Property Redress Scheme, on whose advisory council I sit. The Property Redress Scheme received a 62% increase in complaints about letting agents last year.

The government is currently consulting the industry in relation to possibly having a single ombudsman scheme overseeing the whole of the private rented sector. It has also said that, in future, landlords themselves will need to belong to a redress scheme.

As letting agent regulation is due to become mandatory, I would only use a letting agent who:

1. Is a member of a trade association
2. Has up-to-date Client Money Protection, which is due to be a legal requirement from 1st April 2019 (members of the above associations will get this included in their membership)

3. Carries out the check-in as part of their 'let only' or 'full management' service at no extra cost
4. Uses an inventory clerk who's a member of the Association of Independent Inventory Clerks (AIIC) or the Association of Professional Inventory Providers (APIP) (if they don't have an in-house clerk)
5. Has a good record of managing any tenant/landlord disputes.

Questions to ask

You should already have asked for all the information you require from tenants and agents prior to the check-in, but you should also ask your tenants to confirm they understand they can't do these key things:

1. Move people into the property without notifying you as, by law you have to check tenants have a Right to Rent in the UK
2. Have pets in the home, unless you have granted permission in the tenancy agreement
3. Smoke inside the home
4. Disable any fire safety systems
5. Carry out any works on the property without your approval – including redecoration.

These apply to most agreements these days, although you may choose to allow some of them, which should be clarified in writing.

••

Hot Tip

OUTSOURCE OPTION: An independent inventory clerk can also carry out the check-in if you don't want to instruct an agent. Check they're a member of the AIIC or APIP.

CHAPTER 28
MAKE SURE YOU GET THE INVENTORY MANAGEMENT RIGHT

The Association of Independent Inventory Clerks has called on the government to introduce mandatory independent third-party inventories to help raise standards in the lettings industry.

Besides the tenancy agreement, inventory management reports have become the most important documents required at the start of a tenancy.

They're your evidence of the exact contents and condition of the property when the tenant moves in and if you don't have that evidence, you can't prove that any subsequent damage or theft was down to the tenant.

Inventory management reports include:

- Inventory and schedule of condition
- Check-in – agreement of the inventory by the tenant
- Periodic visits - checking the tenant is meeting the tenancy agreement obligations
- Check out and dilapidation reports - the report that determines change, whether there is damage, cleanliness, missing items, maintenance or general wear and tear.

As Nick Lyons, CEO at No Letting Go, one of the UK's largest inventory companies states, "Disputes are determined at the start of a tenancy, not the end." Accurate and detailed paperwork at the start will not only save you lots of potential headaches when the tenant leaves, but will also send a message to the tenant from the outset that this is what you expect from them.

You may think carrying out an inventory is a simple procedure – simply list the contents and state of the décor, noting any marks or damage. But the reality is, it's not that straightforward and, in my experience, not many landlords have the skills to do the job properly!

Some people think you only need an inventory for furnished properties or ones that have high-value fixtures and fittings, but that couldn't be further from the truth.

It's worth remembering that the biggest costs relate to voids and many voids between tenancies are the result of delays caused by tenant damage or misuse.

A proper inventory (and schedule of condition) should contain both detailed descriptions and photographs and can easily run to 40 or 50 pages. If you want to make sure you can claim money from a tenant who causes damage to your property, the inventory needs to be able to stand up in court, so it really needs to be as professional as possible and preferably prepared by an independent company.

The inventory should be carried out at the start of the tenancy, either on check-in day or just before, gone through with the tenant during check-in and signed, then used at the end of the tenancy when the tenant moves out, to support findings, whether they're chargeable or not. If you send a PDF version or leave a hard copy with the incoming tenants to go through more thoroughly in their own time, they must sign and date it within an agreed fixed period (usually a few days) of moving in. Not ensuring this is done is a key mistake made by many landlords.

As well as being used in case of a dispute, a successful inventory can also help you to avoid a dispute in the first place. For example, if the tenant is disputing paying for damage at any point and you have an inventory they signed and dated on check-in – especially one with photos – you can show them evidence right away that the damage wasn't there when they moved in. This can save you having to dispute the return of the deposit at the end of the tenancy.

The government deposit schemes, which adjudicate against loss caused at the end of a tenancy, recommend landlords have these types of evidence:

1. A robust tenancy agreement in place that refers to your inventory and outlines what is required.

2. A clear, detailed and professional inventory with a schedule of condition.

3. The tenant's signature on the check-in inventory.

4. A comprehensive check-out report, preferably with the tenants on site.

5. Proof that the process of checking in and out is impartial and that audit trails are kept.

6. Reports prepared in text format, with photos or video footage as supporting evidence only.

7. Records of receipts, invoices, estimates, quotations and especially records of cleaning charges, as these are often challenged.

8. Records of all communication.

9. In addition, both the main inventory bodies, the AIIC and APIP, highly recommend that you or your inventory clerk/company:

- Outline the legal requirements of the tenant within the body of the report and include any disclaimers
- Outline your definitions of what is clean and in good condition
- Detail all the areas the tenant is responsible for, including any outbuildings, garage and loft areas

- Reference the condition of items clearly, specifying location, size and description
- Always include brand names and model numbers of appliances
- Take the time to go through the inventory with the tenant and amend any areas that need clarification.

Key steps

1. **Book the inventory just before or on the day of move-in**
   Organise for the inventory to be carried out just prior to handing over the property to the tenant – never after the tenant has already moved in.

2. **Ensure all areas are detailed**
   Make sure every area of the property that the tenant will be occupying or responsible for is covered by the inventory, including front and back gardens, any outbuildings and the driveway.

3. **Include all fixtures and fittings**
   Make sure every item and its condition is detailed, including units, appliances and soft furnishings.

4. **Register keys – types and numbers**

5. **Take meter readings**
   Readings of all utilities should also be included on the inventory: gas, electric and water meters, plus any oil tank readings.

6. **Give the tenant a copy**
   Once you've been through it together, give the tenant a copy of the inventory and make sure they understand it forms part of the tenancy agreement.

7. **Have the tenant agree/sign the inventory**

8. **Check the tenant out against the inventory and any additional check-in documentation**
The tenant has the right to be present, although doesn't have to be there. If you're using an independent inventory provider, it's less important but still preferable.

9. **Properly document any damage**
Ensure you document all damage, missing items, poor cleanliness or poorly-maintained gardens on a check-out report before you make them good, otherwise you may not be able to claim all repair costs from the outgoing tenant.

Who to work with

If you're confident you can carry out the inventory yourself, you can buy 'off the shelf' inventory packages, in both hard copy and digital format, including downloadable inventory templates and software that you can use on Apple and Android smartphones or tablets.

However, it will save you a great deal of time and hassle if you outsource your inventory process to an independent specialist. They can be an excellent member of your team and can provide you with a great deal of expertise and advice, plus you have the added protection of the work being carried out by someone completely impartial.

Choose a company or individual who is a member of a scheme under which they have to abide by a code of practice and you have an independent third party to complain to, if necessary. The two main organisations are the Association of Independent Inventory Clerks (theaiic.co.uk) and The Association of Professional Inventory Providers (apip.org.uk/). The AIIC is not-for-profit and the APIP is part of a larger member organisation for property professionals. Both offer a free helpline to answer your queries about inventories.

Inventories can cost anywhere from £60 to several hundred pounds, depending on the size of the property, furnishings and your location.

Check-outs cost a little less, but overall the cost is easily outweighed by the savings and benefits.

Questions to ask an inventory clerk

1. What training have they received?
2. Can they show you copies of recent inventories?
3. Do they take photos and/or videos to accompany the written document?
4. How do they solve a dispute over the inventory between you and the tenant?
5. What percentage of their inventories have been used for court cases or to solve disputes?
6. In how many/what percentage of cases have their inventories won (and lost)?
7. What would happen if there were a dispute between you and the inventory clerk?
8. How much do they charge for a check-in and check-out inventory?
9. How quickly can they produce the report?
10. Will it be both electronic and hard copy?
11. Do they offer any additional services, such as periodic checks and check-ins/outs?
12. Do they provide advice and support if a dispute arises?

Hot Tip

ADDITIONAL SERVICES. Ask your local independent inventory clerk about other services they provide. Some will also conduct check-ins and outs, carry out periodic checks and even hold a set of keys in case of an emergency, or if tradesmen need access.

PART THREE

RUNNING YOUR PORTFOLIO THE RIGHT WAY

CHAPTER 29
TOP 10 LANDLORD
MAINTENANCE MISTAKES

In a report published in July 2017, Citizens Advice found that 41% of tenants had waited an unreasonably long time – based on national accreditation timescales – for repairs that their landlord was legally required to undertake.

Let's be very clear: the vast majority of landlords will deal with disrepair issues very quickly but problems can occur and, in many cases, they stem from communication issues, on both sides.

Tenants often don't report maintenance issues quickly enough, and landlords don't always prioritise their tenants' requests. What a landlord may see as a "reasonable" response time may be considered excessive by a tenant who may have had no hot water for three days.

Landlords need to prioritise the type of request; a broken boiler or hot water issue should be dealt with immediately, and are more urgent than a broken tile or some grouting in the bathroom. Of course, cost comes into it and landlords can be tempted to cut corners, which can end up with the relationship being jeopardised. Tenants could even decide to withhold rent… even though they are not legally entitled to do so.

Some tenants can be very pedantic and will complain about everything, no matter how petty and regardless of whether it is your responsibility or theirs. In case the tenant decides to make a complaint, make sure all correspondence and time frames are documented, so you can show that necessary repairs were dealt with in a timely manner.

You should not serve a Section 21 notice on a tenant just because they have complained about disrepair. Studies found that 2% of landlords had tried to evict tenants who had complained about maintenance, so the government made it illegal to do this under the Deregulation Act 2015.

Remember: your property is your investment. It is in your interests to protect your investment and sustain the tenant in your property as long as possible.

Mistake 1: Trying to do it all yourself
The first key error with maintenance is not knowing when it's okay to DIY and when you need a qualified tradesman. In my view, you should leave most maintenance to the experts, unless you're in the trade yourself or have experience of upgrading properties. While you're probably perfectly capable of fixing a loose drawer handle, tackling the wiring behind a light switch is a job for a qualified electrician.

Mistake 2: Tatty décor
Good tenants want to rent good-looking properties that are clearly well maintained and cared for. Flaky paint, part-painted pipes, tatty skirting boards or just a bad paint job will put them off the moment they walk in.

Cheap paint is cheap for a reason – it doesn't last – so buy good quality paint that can easily be wiped down and make sure whoever's doing the decorating uses decent brushes and rollers. As soon as the paintwork starts to look less than fresh, give it a new coat.

Remember, if it looks like you're not bothered about the property, you'll attract tenants who won't care for it either. And if your property gets into a rough state, you'll suffer with higher voids and find it hard to keep rents in line with inflation.

Mistake 3: Tatty kitchen and bathrooms
Although it's no secret that decent kitchens and bathrooms are high on tenants' wish lists, a surprising number of landlords allow their units and

fittings to become tired. These areas are the most important parts of the property to keep clean and hygienic and even something like failing sealant around the edge of a bath can make the whole bathroom feel a bit dirty.

Keeping on top of this doesn't have to be expensive. Good kitchen units can be updated with new doors and worktops every five years or so, and even new hinges and handles on existing doors can make them look great. Bathrooms can have a basic but good-quality bathroom suite, with tiled walls and a linoleum floor that's cost-effective and easy to replace.

It's not expensive to get someone in to apply sealant professionally – a good job should last for years without mould growth – or you could go on a course to learn how to do it yourself! The important thing is that you regularly refresh what can be easily done and make sure you have a thorough professional clean between lets.

Mistake 4: Not replacing worn carpets – especially on the stairs
Because new carpeting is one of the bigger periodical costs, landlords often try to get tenants to pay for at least part of it, but unless there has been specific damage, replacing worn and frayed carpets is your responsibility. Take advice from your carpet fitter as to how long you can expect carpets to last in reasonable condition and budget accordingly for replacements – don't allow them to get 'old'.

It's particularly important you make regular checks on any stair carpet. One of the requirements for your property to pass the Housing Health and Safety Rating System is that the carpet on the stairs is properly attached and there are no rips and tears that could cause someone to trip or fall.

Mistake 5: Lack of attention to electrics
Too many landlords happily sign off that the electrics are all fine. If the property is new or less than five years old and hasn't had too many tenants in it, it should be okay. However, you don't know what tenants might have been up to or fiddled with, and electrics can deteriorate over time.

For around £100 you can have a Part P qualified electrician carry out an Electrical Installation Condition Report and give you a certificate to confirm the state of the wiring and safety of the electrical system. Five-year checks are to become mandatory but it is recommended you carry this out every 3-5 years or after each tenancy.

Mistake 6: Not renewing gas safety certificates on time

Not only is it a legal requirement to have an annual gas safety check, it's a moral obligation to take every possible step to ensure the safety of your tenants. Landlords sometimes allow their certificates to lapse, often because it can be a hassle trying to organise a time for either the tenant to be in or to get to the property themselves to give the engineer access.

The fact is, it's not the tenant's responsibility to be there for works required, so you must either make time yourself or have someone you trust let in the Gas Safe registered professional. Diarise the annual renewal date and book the appointment in good time. Thanks to a change in the law in April 2018, organising a gas safety check is now easier as you can arrange it for up to two months before it expires without losing out on your full 12 months of certification.

TIP: It is a legal requirement to provide a carbon monoxide detector in any room used as living accommodation which has a solid fuel appliance. But these rules are being reviewed by the government later in 2018 and it is good practice to install one where there is a gas appliance, too. You can pick one up for under £20 and it could help save your tenants' lives. As with a smoke alarm, it should be tested and confirmed to be working at the start of the tenancy.

Mistake 7: Not fixing leaking taps, pipes or radiators

'Minor' leaks are all too often ignored or considered low priority by both landlords and tenants. But a dripping tap can quickly turn into several buckets of water being wasted on a daily basis and radiator leaks can ruin a good carpet or other flooring with horrid black or dark brown liquid. Both will ultimately result in damage to your property and a very unhappy tenant, so deal with leaks as soon as you become aware of them.

During check-in, periodic checks and check out, make sure you look at the property's pipework and taps to make sure everything 's in good working order. And remind your tenant on check-in that you'd appreciate a call as soon as they notice any problems.

Mistake 8: Not keeping guttering and drains clear
It's easy to forget about exterior guttering and pipework, but you must to keep it clear and make sure none of the joints is leaking. If you allow drains to become blocked by vegetation or tree roots, or guttering to fill up with leaves and moss from the roof, your property walls will soon become damp. That, in turn, will cause mould on your interior décor and can lead to a horrible smell, both of which will drive tenants away.

It costs less than a few hundred pounds to have all your gutters thoroughly cleared out – a good local contractor or handyman may do it for less – and you should arrange to have it carried out annually, as well as making careful checks after any heavy storms.

Mistake 9: Ignoring damp
Damp is one of the main issues for landlords and a pet hate of tenants. Properties built more than a hundred years ago – as many private rented properties were - are susceptible to damp and may need the damp course redoing. A properly injected damp proof course should last for 20 years, so it's worth doing properly.

Tenants are often alarmed by surface mould and may call to report 'damp'. Nine times out of ten, it is the result of condensation caused, for example, by them drying washing and other damp clothing in the house, or taking hot showers without ventilating the property properly. That may be fixed by wiping down paintwork and spraying with anti-mould treatment; however there may be a bigger problem which requires you to install ventilation or it may be that there is damp due to structural issues. Always get a professional diagnosis as damp is not allowed in a property and you could face hefty fines.

mydeposits has produced a report on damp and mould which you can read here: https://www.mydeposits.co.uk/wp-content/uploads/Understanding-Damp-Mould-1.pdf

Mistake 10: Not checking roof tiles
Roofs are easy to forget about, because we can't see them very well! However, heavy wind, rain and snow can easily displace tiles, so make sure you check on the state of your roof every six months or so and after any storms. Pop your head into the loft during the day to see if there's any sunlight shining through and, if there is, it doesn't cost much to get a competent roofer to replace the tiles; choose one from an organisation such as the Confederation of Roofing Contractors.

Whatever you do, don't ignore missing tiles, as water can quickly get in and rot the timbers, which will cost a lot more to fix.

And one more thing to bear in mind…
Tenanted properties can be great targets for criminals, so make sure all the locks – including windows, doors and for outbuildings – are kept in good condition and the tenant knows how to keep the property properly secured so that, if anything happens, the insurance company will pay out.

Key steps

1. **Check the survey**
   Go through the survey you had when you bought the property and see what areas need attention, both now and in the future.

2. **Have a checklist**
   Note down likely problems and know where to look for them – from water leaks, to wear and tear, to electrical and gas or carbon monoxide leaks – so you can carry out regular checks efficiently.

3. **Know the cost v benefit of using professionals**
   Check the cost of having a professional carry out maintenance work and what guarantees they give, versus the cost of doing it yourself. It's usually well worth letting qualified contractors carry out maintenance. Use contractors who give warranties and guarantees for their work, and ideally who are insured to cover costs even if they go bust.

4. **Keep a schedule of works**
   Keep a record of all work undertaken and schedule in when it's likely to need checking or doing again.

5. **File all paperwork carefully**
   Keep all guarantees and certificates in a safe place so you can lay your hands on them easily, if required, and file your receipts properly so your accountant can allocate costs correctly and mitigate your tax liability.

Who to work with

Any reputable contractor or tradesman will be a member of a recognised or licensed trade organisation. Importantly, gas engineers need to be on the Gas Safe Register, electricians should be Part P registered, glaziers should be FENSA registered and builders should be members of the Federation of Master Builders.

You can find good local tradespeople onTrustmark.org.uk, all of whom work to government-endorsed standards and Propertychecklists.co.uk offers free lists of 'to dos' for maintenance, so you can make sure you get jobs done correctly with the best professionals.

Be aware that many cowboys will falsify their membership of these organisations, so check their member status online or give the organisation a call.

Questions to ask tradespeople

1. Which organisation are you a member of?
2. How long have you been a member?
3. What training have you had and how many years in the trade?
4. How much will the job cost?
5. How long will it take?
6. Do you clear up afterwards?
7. What guarantees come with the work?
8. What if there's a problem after the job's been completed?
9. Can you separate labour and parts in your quote and invoice?
10. What insurance do you have and will it cover accidents during the job on the property?

Hot Tip

DON'T PAY IN CASH. Lots of tradespeople will give you a reduced price 'for cash', but they may not give you all the receipts and guarantees and, should anything go wrong, you may not be able to claim against them. Without proper invoices, you may also not be able to deduct the cost of works from a tax perspective or defend yourself against any accusations of lack of repairs.

CHAPTER 30
DEALING WITH INSURANCE CLAIMS

We all hate paying out for insurance... until something goes wrong and we need to claim! And, as a landlord, you need to ensure you have specialist insurance that will cover you for accidental damage by tenants – and their friends – as well as the property itself, fixtures and fittings and appliances.

It's important that both you and your tenant know what to do if something happens that means you need to make an insurance claim, so that there's no sudden frantic search for paperwork.

If your insurance was organised through a third party, such as a letting agent or a landlord association, their service may include contacting the insurance company and organising the necessary works, in which case it may be that you simply need to call them.

In any case, when you have an incident, it's always worth contacting your insurance company or broker directly right away – they may cover things you don't realise and, even if they don't, they'll be able to advise you about what steps to take and may have access to good tradespeople.

Key steps

1. **Have all the relevant information when you call your insurer:**
   - Your policy details
   - The property address and postcode
   - If it's a break-in, you'll need a police crime reference number
   - Brief description of the insurance claim
   - Any photos to help show the damage
   - Have a notepad ready to take down any references, instructions, numbers to call, etc.

2. **Complete a claim form**
   Most insurance companies will take the details from you via a call, then email or have you download your claim form, to be checked, completed, signed and returned.

3. **Visit from a loss adjuster**
   If it's a big claim, for example after a fire, then your insurer might have to send a loss adjuster out to assess the damage more thoroughly prior to settling.

4. **Payment received**
   Once the claim has been agreed, the insurer should send you a cheque to cover the loss. In some cases, they may send out vouchers for you to purchase damaged items from certain places they have an agreement with.

5. **Replace/repair**
   Carry out the works required, making sure you have any works carried out by reputable tradespeople and retain all receipts and invoices.

6. **Check insurance cover**
   Once any repairs have been carried out, check that any improvements or substitute items, as well as the up-to-date rebuild value, are fully covered by your policy.

Who to work with

All landlord insurance has to be offered by companies who abide by Financial Services Ombudsman rules and regulations, so most of them are reasonable companies to deal with.

Ideally, choose a specialist insurance company that has experience of dealing specifically with landlord and tenant claims. They'll understand the key claims you're likely to have to make and charge a premium accordingly.

If you choose to go with the cheapest quote, go through the paperwork very carefully, to make sure you're properly covered. 'Good deals' often only cover you for the absolute minimum, rather than what you're actually likely to need to claim for.

The key is to pick a company that offers comprehensive insurance at a competitive price. We work with Hamilton Fraser, so feel free to give them a call on 0345 310 6300 for a quote.

Questions to ask

You want to work with an insurance company that will give you one point of contact and manage your claim efficiently, so you can sort things out as quickly as possible for both you and your tenant.

So, when you call with your claim, ask:

1. If it's completely covered by your insurance
2. If it's covered by any other insurance you have with the company
3. What will happen once they've taken the information from you
4. Whether there will be one person allocated to your case for you to liaise with
5. How long it's likely to take for the claim to be processed
6. Whether you have to use any particular recommended tradespeople or are able to choose your own
7. If you need to provide quotes or receipts for the work and, if so, in what format
8. Whether the claim will increase your insurance and, if so, by how much
9. How the monies will be paid – by cheque, vouchers or BACS
10. What your claim reference is for future contact.

Hot Tip

TAKE PICTURES. Don't rush to clear up until you've carefully photographed all damage, and/or taken video footage. You should write everything down as well, but a picture tells a thousand words.

CHAPTER 31
HOW TO CARRY OUT A PERIODIC PROPERTY INSPECTION

Ideally, carry out a property inspection within a month of the tenant moving in and then every three to six months.

Carrying out inspections on properties seems to be a bit of a problem for landlords that I meet. Many are reluctant to 'bother' their tenants and see it as invading their privacy, but periodically visiting the property is the only way to make sure it's being kept in good order and that the tenants aren't breaching any terms.

The inspection doesn't need to be very long – you can usually see pretty quickly if there's anything that needs to be addressed – but make sure you pay attention to:

- Any signs of smoking or pets if not allowed in the contract
- Areas that may be susceptible to leaks
- What security measures the tenants are taking (does it look like they're complying with insurance requirements?)
- General cleanliness.
- If there are more people living there than on the tenancy agreement

If the property is messy and doesn't look as though it's cleaned very often, that's usually a sign your tenants don't really care about it, so you might want to spend a little longer there, checking that the mess isn't hiding any stains or other damage.

Take the opportunity to talk to the tenant, ask if they have any questions and make sure everything's working okay for them. There may be something very minor that you haven't picked up, and that they may not have wanted to bother you with – perhaps something like a dripping tap – but you want to keep everything in good working order, so make sure they know they can mention even the slightest thing. It helps build trust with the tenant and gives them confidence that their landlord cares. And if there are any issues, you can get to them early before they become a real and costly problem.

Key steps

You can carry out periodic checks yourself or pay someone else to do them – if you're under full management with an agent, they'll do them for you. Either way, make sure the tenant has been advised in writing at the start of the tenancy that you'll be organising regular visits and that these benefit you both.

1. **Inform the tenant.**
   Check the minimum notice you need to give to access the property and advise the tenant in writing, eg by email, that you'd like to arrange to visit.

2. **Make an appointment.**
   Agree a day and time when the tenant can be there, ideally when it's light.

   NOTE: you have to have the tenants' consent to attend at an appointed time. If they fail to respond to you by phone or email, you cannot just attend and let yourself in; that can be construed as harassment.

3. **Take the inventory.**
   Take along the inventory report so you can compare condition/damage.

4. **Talk to the tenant.**
   Sit down with the tenant and ask if there's anything that needs fixing and whether they have any other queries.

5. **Inspect the inside.**
   Check the condition of the interior and if there's any post lying around, check it belongs to the tenant. If not, it may be a sign they are subletting.

6. **Inspect the outside.**
   Look around the outside of the property to make sure there are no leaks or drain issues and check any outbuildings are secure.

7. **Agree what the tenant needs to do.**
   Discuss with the tenant anything they need to do, such as clean the cooker or keep the garden tidier.

8. **Agree what you need to do.**
   Confirm what you'll do, such as fix a leak or ask the council to supply a larger rubbish bin.

9. **Put everything agreed in writing to the tenant.**

10. **Carry out works.**
    Implement everything you've promised to do and keep any guarantees or receipts for the work. Don't forget you must respond to tenant requests for repairs within 14 days.

Who to work with

Agents and inventory clerks are experienced in carrying out inspections and can do a great job of checking the property over for you. If you have a fully-managed service, the agent should carry out checks every three to six months and let you have a copy of their report.

It's particularly good if you can get the same person who carried out the original inventory to do the periodic check, as they'll be familiar with any potential problems and should be able to spot any change in condition more quickly.

Questions to ask

When you're using an agent to carry out a periodic check, make sure you ask them:

1. How often do they carry out periodic checks?
2. Is this included in the cost of management?
3. What's the cost of an individual check?
4. How long do they typically spend at the property?
5. Do they take the inventory and check everything against it?
6. Are their reports 'ad hoc' or do they have templates to complete?
7. Do they find out if the tenant is up to date with their utility bills?
8. Do they check the post at the property?
9. Can they confirm the tenant is meeting the security requirements of your insurance company?
10. What action do they take if they find the tenant is breaching their agreement, eg smoking, keeping a pet or sub-letting?

●●

Hot Tip

CHECK TENANTS' PLANS. Take the opportunity to ask, face to face, whether they're happy in the property and whether they plan to stay or move on at the end of the tenancy – it can give you a heads up.

CHAPTER 32
TOP 5 MISTAKES LANDLORDS MAKE WHEN COMMUNICATING (OR NOT!) WITH TENANTS

In my experience, most landlord and tenant issues come from a simple lack of communication.

If you have a good relationship with your tenant, it's less likely you'll have any serious issues during the tenancy. That means you need to communicate properly to build trust, and it's a two-way street.

The average term of a tenancy is two years and four months for 25-34-year-olds and four years and five months for tenants aged 35-44, according to the latest research by Nationwide (June 2018). Older tenants stay even longer, with the over 55s spending an average of six years and nine months in the same rental property.

Remember you want your tenant to stay in your property as long as possible, so let them know from the start that they should call you (or your managing agent) right away if there's anything they're not entirely happy with or if there's a maintenance issue – leaking radiator, loose cupboard door, etc – so you can sort it out for them as quickly as possible before it becomes a big problem. For your part, you need to respond quickly, be clear on what you can and will do about any issues, then keep the tenant updated with what's going to happen and when.

Make it known to them that you see yourself as a professional landlord running a business, but that you are approachable, you understand your obligations and you want to have a good working relationship.

Here are the top five communication mistakes landlords make:

Mistake 1: Not responding to calls quickly enough

This is one of the biggest complaints I hear from tenants. If your tenant calls with a problem, you need to call them back as soon as possible, even if it's something you consider minor – nobody likes to feel ignored!

Unfortunately, people often have different ideas of how long is a 'reasonable' timeframe to respond: an hour... four hours... a day... so agree with your tenant right at the start of their tenancy what both of you think is reasonable, and stick to it.

Mistake 2: Not being clear about how long the property is available for rent

If your property is going to be available for a long time, let tenants know; if it's only going to be free for six months or a year, be fair and tell your tenants at the start. It's really important to try and find a tenant that matches your own requirements, otherwise you could end up with bad feeling for the remainder of the tenancy and you might have to fight them to leave.

Mistake 3: Not explaining your right of access

While it's the tenant's responsibility to read the tenancy agreement and make sure they understand what they're signing, you should explain what your access rights to the property are and about the periodic checks you'll need to make. You must make sure your tenant understands that, although they're renting the property, they don't have the exclusive right to it.

Mistake 4: Not making it clear who's responsible for what jobs within the property

A lot of tenants haven't spent much time renting or even living on their own before, so you must make sure you explain what you can and will do to help them and what they need to do themselves. It never ceases to amaze me how many tenants expect their landlords to change a light bulb!

Mistake 5: Getting it wrong when arranging access for tradespeople

Many landlords forget that if there's something wrong with the property they're letting, it's their responsibility, not the tenant's, to be there to let tradespeople in. Bear in mind, it may take several visits to assess the situation, fit the parts and check everything's working properly, so make sure you let your tenant know when these visits are taking place and that you'll be there to provide access. If you have a good relationship and the tenant is available, they may agree to be there themselves, even though they don't legally have to.

Key steps

1. **Be clear from the start**
    Start as you mean to go on: talk to the tenant about the renting process, explain rights and responsibilities, make sure you're both clear on how and when you'll communicate. Tenants in England should be given a copy of the government's How to Rent Guide (www.gov.uk/government/publications/how-to-rent), as this is a legal requirement.

2. **Exchange contact details**
    Whether you're managing yourself or using an agent, it's important the tenant can contact you/your agent by phone and email with general queries and maintenance issues. And make sure you have the tenant's email, mobile and work number so you can always reach them.

3. **Be clear on emergencies**
    Make sure your tenant knows what to do in case of an emergency, such as a fire, theft, flood or storm damage – both who to call and what steps to take themselves. Get a next of kin or parent telephone number in case of emergency. You may also wish to take out Landlord Home Emergency Cover for your property.

4. **Manage expectations**
    Let your tenant know you will always address problems quickly but that tradespeople aren't hanging around all day waiting for your call!

During busy periods it can take up to a week to get a tradesperson out and potentially longer to get the problem fixed.

5. **Put everything in writing**
   Always confirm everything in writing to the tenant, so you have a clear record in case there's a future dispute

Who to work with

Even if you use a letting agent to manage the property and tenant, you should still check in with the tenant every now and then to make sure they're being looked after properly and getting a good service from the agent. Apart from being good business practice, it's also self-preservation – a happy tenant is more likely to pay rent on time and look after your investment!

And don't ever choose a letting agent based purely on the commission or fee they charge. Always go with a self-regulated agent that offers the best service, otherwise the few pounds you save on a cheaper option could lose you thousands during the tenancy, through voids and fixing problems.

Questions to ask

When you engage a letting agent to look after your tenant, it's important they're not only responsive, but also proactive. So ask them:

1. How many tenant complaints do they have annually?
2. Do they have many tenancy deposit disputes?
3. Will the tenant have a dedicated point of contact?
4. Do they monitor the time it takes to get back to tenants via email and/or telephone?
5. How quickly do the tradespeople they use tend to be able to carry out work?

6. If they operate an out of hours service, how qualified are the staff to answer tenant queries?
7. Do they have an answering machine if everyone is out of the office?
8. What holiday cover do they have?
9. Do they have a code of conduct for communicating with landlords and tenants?
10. Do they give you regular reports of how the tenancy is going and communication with the tenant?

• •

Hot Tip

TAKE RESPONSIBILITY FOR COMMUNICATION. It can make or break a tenancy so, even if you employ a letting agent, make the effort to ensure everyone's communicating effectively and the tenant is happy with the service they're getting.

CHAPTER 33
MOVING A TENANT OUT SUCCESSFULLY

The English Housing Survey 2016-17 found the main reasons tenants leave their rental property is due to their job, to move to a larger property or to a better neighbourhood. Only 10% of tenancies are ended by landlords.

There are many perfectly valid reasons for your tenant wanting to leave. They could be moving in with a partner, have got a new job in a different area, or they may have decided to buy their own home and, in these cases, there probably isn't anything you can do to change their minds.

However, there may be another reason for them giving notice that you could address, so always ask the agent or the tenant directly why they want to leave.

If it's because there are some problems with the property that the tenant simply hasn't brought up, such as a weak shower or a dodgy washing machine, you may be able to persuade them to stay by spending a few hundred pounds. And if they're a good tenant, who looks after the property and always pays rent on time, it's worth trying to keep them.

Whatever money you spend on the property will help maintain its value and could well be a lot cheaper than incurring voids and re-letting fees.

But, assuming the tenant is leaving, the most important thing to consider first is the paperwork, which you have to get right from the start.

If it's the tenant who's chosen to move out, then they should have given you formal notice – in writing and at the correct time, as set out in the tenancy agreement (usually one or two months) – of the day they're moving out. If they've given you less notice, you have to make a judgement call as to whether you hold them to paying any outstanding rent for the full period of the agreement, or allow them some leeway. If they've been renting from you for a long time, looked after your property and you can easily re-let, then it might be worth letting them off.

The rules and tenancy agreement in Scotland are different. You can read more in Chapter 5.

If it's your decision for the tenant to leave, you MUST make sure you give them the correct notice, which will depend on why you're asking them to go. Is it because of non-payment of rent or some other breach of agreement, or do you want the property back because you need to live in it yourself? (See later chapters on sections 8 and 21). If you don't issue the paperwork in the right order, at the right time, the notice may be considered invalid and you'll have the start the process all over again and may struggle to evict them if they refuse to leave.

The other potentially contentious issue is the deposit. The process of returning the deposit to a tenant will be set out by the protection scheme you've used and you'll need to abide by their rules and timeframes. If there's a dispute, there will be a set procedure and requirement for both you and the tenant to give evidence, so make sure you've kept a record of **everything** in writing. (See Chapter 25 on Tenancy Deposit Schemes.)

Key steps

1. **Confirm the end of the tenancy in writing**
   Both you and the tenant need to have it in writing that the tenancy is coming to an end and have issued the correct notices. If you failed

to give your tenant the prescribed information at the start of the tenancy, a notice cannot be served.

2. **Agree the move-out date**

3. **Make sure the tenant has a copy of the inventory**
Ensure the tenant has a copy of the inventory they signed and dated on check-in, so they can check the property against the inventory themselves and work out if anything is damaged or missing.

4. **Make sure the tenant knows what they need to do before they leave**
Check the tenant has an easy-to-read list of what the legal agreement states they have to do before they leave the property.

5. **Confirm cleaning obligations**
Cleaning of the property – and especially the cooker – is often disputed, so check and remind the tenant if their tenancy agreement states they need to use a professional company.

6. **Confirm deposit scheme procedure**
Check your tenancy deposit scheme rules for returning the deposit to your tenant and be aware of any deadlines you or the tenant has to meet. You need to have given your tenant the prescribed information at the beginning of the tenancy, as detailed in Chapter 21, otherwise the deposit protection is invalid.

7. **Utility bills**
Organise with the tenant how the utility bills will be moved over and make sure they don't get them cut off.

8. **Arrange to meet for the check-out**
Agree to meet the tenant on the day at a time when most of their belongings have been moved out.

9. **Take meter readings**
   Make a note of all meter readings on move-out day, ideally taking photos.

10. **Carry out the check-out inventory**
    Check the property's condition matches the check-in inventory description and pictures.

11. **Agree deposit deductions**
    During your meeting with the tenant on check-out day, agree what is wear and tear, what is your responsibility to fix, and what damage that the tenant needs to pay for.

12. **Take a forwarding address for the tenant(s)**

13. **Take back keys**
    Check the tenant gives you back all the keys and don't forget about keys for outbuildings. They should all have been recorded on the check-in inventory.

14. **Return the deposit**
    Organise for the deposit, less any agreed deductions, to be returned to the tenant.

Who to work with

Rather than check out the tenant yourself, you can pay an agent or inventory clerk to do this for you. If you're paying a letting agent for full management, it should be included in their service at no extra cost.

Ideally, even if you've engaged an agent, you should meet with them and the tenant on move-out day. You may think this is 'doubling up' but I'd suggest it's time well spent, ensuring that all three of you agree that everything's as it should be, so you avoid any differences of opinion after the event.

For example, the tenant might not have kept the garden as neat and tidy as you expected they would, but the letting agent might not see this as a major problem. If the tenant is checked out and their deposit returned before you see the garden for yourself, you could end up in a dispute with the agent.

While you're there, you can also discuss with the letting agent about what work is required to re-let the property.

Questions to ask

If your letting agent is carrying out the check-out, you should find out the following from them, to ensure the property can be re-let as soon as possible:

1. Did the tenant give the correct amount of notice?
2. Have all the keys been returned?
3. Whose responsibility is it to return the deposit?
4. Have the utilities, council tax and other services been alerted to the move?
5. Is there anything missing or any damage from the tenancy?
6. Does the property need any further work to re-let it?
7. What are the estimated costs of upgrading the property?
8. How long will it take to re-let the property?
9. Are there any costs associated with re-letting the property?
10. Do you expect to get more or less rent when you re-let?

. . . .

Hot Tip

BE REASONABLE. Use your common sense when it comes to holding tenants precisely to their notice period and deciding what's wear and tear and what's damage. Disputes can take a lot of time and are a lot of hassle, so avoid them if you can.

CHAPTER 34
RETURNING THE DEPOSIT: WHAT TO KEEP; WHAT NOT TO KEEP

In the year to March 2018, the most common cause of a deposit dispute was cleaning, which made up a quarter of all disputes. This was followed by damage and redecoration, according to mydeposits.

The deposit may only seem a small amount to you, but it's a significant amount of money to most tenants. They may have very few savings and, if they're moving to another rental property, are likely to need to use the deposit they're getting back from you for the new one. But before you give the tenant all of their deposit back, make sure they're returning the property to you in the same condition in which you originally let it to them.

The key to dealing with deposits is to be fair and reasonable over any deductions you want to make. Bear in mind that if you haven't put your deposit into a scheme, you may not be able to evict your tenant via the courts and the tenant could make a claim against you if you're found to be breaking the law.

Tenancy deposit schemes rules and regulations
All the various deposit schemes have different rules and regulations when it comes to returning the deposit to your tenant, agreeing any deductions or putting the deposit into dispute. Make sure you're up to date with these so if there are any problems you know how to deal with them.

Most of the information you need about the tenancy deposit scheme will be included in the tenancy agreement and all the schemes detail their processes online. If you have any queries or doubts about what to do and when, you can email or call them.

What you can't deduct from the deposit

There will inevitably be wear and tear, especially if the tenants have been living there for a while, and you can't deduct money from the deposit to pay for what is simply natural deterioration of the property. Wear and tear is typically things like small nicks and scratches on paintwork, worn carpets and curtains and a bit of mould in bathrooms/kitchens.

What you can deduct from the deposit

Where the tenant has caused damage, you can agree with them directly, or via dispute resolution with the tenancy deposit scheme, to deduct money from the deposit. Examples of damage include holes in walls or plaster, cracked window panes, stains or burns on carpets, missing items and a poorly-cleaned oven or property. Make sure you take photographs as well as written descriptions of the damage, in case there is a dispute.

Evidence required if a dispute arises

If the tenant disagrees with your assessment, you need to be able to prove that the damage was caused during their tenancy, so it's vital you have a thorough inventory taken at check-in (see Chapter 28). Photos and written descriptions that clearly show the damage wasn't there when the tenant took over the property, signed off by the tenant on check-in, should be enough to support your claim.

All tenancy deposit schemes will have deadlines you need to meet for lodging a dispute and submitting evidence.

Transferring deposit monies back to the tenant

If you're happy to return the deposit in full and are with an insurance-based scheme, it's down to you to return the money to the tenant. You need to do this before the deadline set by the scheme – typically within 10 days of the tenant leaving the property. If you're using a custodial scheme, once they have received your instruction to return the deposit they should do this for you. If you and the tenant have agreed any deductions, the tenant must also confirm to the custodial scheme that they're happy with the amount you've proposed.

Key steps

1. **Confirm who's dealing with the deposit**
   Contact your letting agent to check whether they will handle the return of the deposit or whether you'll have to administer it yourself.

2. **Locate all the details**
   If you're dealing with the deposit yourself, check you have all the details, including any reference numbers and passwords.

3. **Agree how much of the deposit is to be returned**
   Agree with the tenant how much of the deposit they'll get back and put in writing what any deductions relate to.

4. **Confirm the amount to the tenancy deposit scheme**
   Both you and the tenant need to advise the tenancy deposit scheme, either in writing or via their online process, the amount you have both agreed should be paid back.

5. **The deposit should be repaid by the scheme within 10 days, following approval by landlord and tenant**

6. **Make any insurance-based scheme repayment yourself**
   If you kept the deposit money under an insurance-based scheme, you will have to refund the tenant yourself within the required timeframe. You will need the tenant's bank details and a forwarding address.

7. **Submit evidence in any dispute**
   In case of a dispute, make sure you submit any evidence within the required timeframe - usually 28 days.

8. **Be reasonable**
   Be fair with the amount you want to deduct from the deposit to aid a speedy resolution.

Who to work with

mydeposits has been protecting deposits for 11 years and is now used by 150,000 landlords. Backed by the National Landlords Association and run by buy-to-let insurance experts Hamilton Fraser, mydeposits insures more than 908,000 deposits per year, protecting a further 80,000 deposits in its custodial scheme.

In the financial year to 31st March 2018:

- 50% of disputes resulted in a split decision, favouring the tenant
- 18% resulted in a split decision favouring the landlord
- 1% resulted in an equal split
- 25% resulted in a full award to the tenant
- 6% resulted in a full award to the landlord

Questions to ask a tenancy deposit scheme provider

1. What information, help and guidance do they give you?
2. What percentage of awards do they make to landlords versus tenants?
3. If it's a custodial scheme, how long will it take to return the deposit to the tenant?
4. Will there be any costs involved in settling a dispute?
5. What evidence is required for a dispute?
6. Within how many days do you have to provide evidence for a dispute?
7. How do they calculate deposit awards?
8. If the tenant is moving to another of your properties, can you transfer the deposit?
9. Do they have a helpline?
10. What happens if either you or the tenant disputes their decision?

Hot Tip

DATE STAMP EVIDENCE OF DAMAGE. Make sure there is some proof that the damage was recorded at check out and therefore couldn't have been caused after the tenant had left. Upload your photos and/or written description online immediately, or (preferably) have the tenant sign to confirm what you've recorded.

CHAPTER 35
TOP 5 REASONS LANDLORDS FAIL TO NOTICE THE TENANT HASN'T PAID THEIR RENT

Make sure the tenant's rent day is flagged in your diary, for you to check payment. It never ceases to amaze me how many landlords – and even some letting agents – don't check if the tenant has paid their rent on time and in full.

Reason 1: Not knowing the date the rent is due
There's really no excuse for this. The date the tenant needs to pay their rent is in the tenancy agreement and you should have a diary reminder to check your bank. Bear in mind that it may take up to five days from when they make the payment for it to show it in your account.

Reason 2: Not having a separate property account
It's not so easy to keep track of rents if you have them paid into your personal bank account; it's far better to have a separate account purely for rental income and to track costs. It's easier to spot when a tenant hasn't paid and makes doing your accounts and tax returns much more straightforward.

Reason 3: Trying to do too much yourself
Some landlords I meet have lots of properties and, to save money, try to do everything themselves. The result is that when things get busy or something happens in their personal life, they get distracted, miss rents not being paid and end up losing more money than it would have cost them to engage a professional.

If you have lots of properties, especially coupled with a full-time job, you need to get help, either from a bookkeeper or a letting agent. Don't forget that their costs are tax deductible, so it could ultimately cost you less than you pay out, thanks to a reduced tax bill.

Reason 4: Being away from home/work
Even if you usually keep a good check on your bank account, when you go on holiday or have to be away from daily duties due to work or illness, missing rental payments can easily go unnoticed. It can be some time later when you eventually realise rent has not been paid, which has meant a big delay in chasing up your tenants.

Reason 5: Not keeping a rent book for weekly payments
If you're collecting rent from tenants on a weekly basis, by law you have to have a rent book that records all payments the tenant makes. If you don't, not only are you breaking the law, but both you and your tenant will end up forgetting what's been paid when and whether the rent is up to date.

Always get the tenant to sign to confirm they've given you their rent, so there can be no disputes.

Key steps

1. **Know the date rent is due**

2. **Have a separate bank account for your property income and expenditure**

3. **Itemise payments made**
   Speak to the bank to see if payments can be itemised or referenced, so you can more easily see which property rental income and outgoings relate to.

4. **Diarise checks**
   Have a list of the dates that rent is due and make sure it's in your account within five days.

5. **Chase the tenant**
   If the tenant hasn't paid, give them a call – it's better to speak to them, rather than text or email.

6. **Get confirmation of payment**
   If the tenant says they've paid, ask them to supply confirmation from their bank.

7. **Investigate where the payment is**
   If the money hasn't arrived in your account within five days of the tenant having made the payment, ask your bank to investigate what's happened.

8. **Review payments before the end of the tenancy**
   Always review all the tenant's rent payments towards the end of the tenancy, so you can resolve any outstanding rent issues prior to them leaving.

9. **Write to the tenant about non-payment**
   If the tenant hasn't paid, send them a letter by recorded delivery, stating the rent they owe and the terms and conditions from the agreement that explains what happens if they don't pay.

10. **Initiate legal notice and eviction processes, if required**

Who to work with

Rather than trying to keep up with rental admin yourself, you can use the rent collection services that most letting agents offer. This costs less than full management and might be worth investigating. You'll still need to manage the tenant and any property problems, but the essential task of making sure your rental income is received on time, in full, on a weekly or monthly basis, can be taken care of by the letting agent instead.

Make sure you choose a good agent who is a member of a trade association and has Client Money Protection so that if anything happens to them – for example, they go bust – their insurance will ensure you still get your rent.

Questions to ask

When choosing a letting agent to help to collect your rent, make sure you ask:

1. Do they have up-to-date Client Money Protection insurance? If they don't, you have to question whether they are worth using as an agent as this will be a legal requirement from 1st April 2019.
2. How do they check rents have been paid?
3. How quickly will you receive your money after the rent has been paid to the letting agent?
4. Who is responsible for chasing the tenant if the rental payment hasn't be made?
5. What percentage of their tenants have had to be evicted for non-payment of rent?

•••

Hot Tip

EMAIL FOLLOW-UP. If you haven't managed to get hold of a tenant to chase late rent, leave a message and then follow it up with an email so there's a record of when you tried to contact them.

•••

Case Study

One of our cases, which featured on the third series of Nightmare Tenants, Slum Landlords, involved Paul Lewis, a landlord friend of mine. Paul had inherited a property from his father who had serious dementia and sadly died. The property was in an expensive part of West London and the tenant stopped paying the rent for two years, taking advantage of the situation. Thankfully, she left after we served a notice and is now repaying the debt in monthly instalments, after the landlord threatened bankruptcy proceedings.

CHAPTER 36
TOP 10 REASONS TENANTS STOP PAYING RENT

Your Move reported that 9.2% of tenancies were in arrears in May 2018, well below the all-time high of 14.6%, which was recorded in February 2010.

Source: Your Move

If a tenant has stopped paying their rent, you must find out the reason, so you can decide whether to try to help them through their difficulties or start eviction proceedings.

Some landlords I speak to talk about evicting tenants as soon as they don't pay – even if they're only a day or two behind – which I think is wrong. Most of us experience financial problems at some point and, as long as the problems are only short term and you can afford to be patient, helping a tenant through a tough time can result in them becoming a loyal tenant for many years.

The government has said it plans to introduce a "breathing space" scheme, similar to the existing Debt Arrangement Scheme in Scotland. Details have not been finalised but the government is considering a system where those in serious debt can apply for "legal protection from further interest, charges and enforcement action for a period of up to six weeks".

When you find out the reason for non-payment, it's likely to be one of the following:

1. Simply forgot!
It's all-too-easy to forget to make payments when you're supposed to, so if the tenant has, suggest they either set up a standing order (by far the best

option for you) or have an electronic diary alert. Make sure they know that it can take up to five days for transfers to go through and the money should reach your bank account on the date specified in the tenancy agreement.

2. Temporary cash flow problems, such as waiting to be paid
It could be that the tenant can't pay you because they're owed money themselves, which can happen when people are living month-to-month. Their wages may not have been paid on time because of a bank holiday, IT glitches or cash flow problems at the company. If they're self-employed, they may just be bad at credit control.

And sometimes bills stack up so much that a tenant can't meet their payment. You need to understand whether this is a one-off problem – such as a big dentist's bill – or whether the tenant is simply poor at managing their finances, in which case, I'm afraid it's likely to keep happening.

3. Believe you're not doing what you should… so why should they?
Lots of evictions I deal with stem from a tenant refusing to pay rent because they say the landlord hasn't fixed a problem or kept up their end of the agreement. Unfortunately for the tenant, that still doesn't give them the legal right to withhold rent. If you're communicating properly with the tenant and meeting your obligations, you shouldn't run into this issue.

4. Delays in receiving Universal Credit
According to the RLA, in September 2017 more than a third of private landlords with tenants receiving Universal Credit were owed rent. The way the benefit is paid can make it more difficult for some tenants to manage their budgets – and there have been well-publicised delays in payments to those switching to the new system. The RLA has called for the government to make it easier and quicker for payments to be made directly to the landlord in cases where arrears are building up. Currently, the landlord can only apply for a "managed payment" (where the rent is paid direct) when the tenant is two months in arrears and, even then, the DWP may decide to offer budgeting advice to the tenant instead. The landlord can also apply for managed payments from day

one if the tenant has specified vulnerabilities; these are known as Tier 1 and Tier 2 factors. This can, however, be quite a lengthy process.

5. Loss of job

Losing their job can quickly result in tenants not being able to pay their rent. It's worth doing what you can to help them apply for benefits if it means they can stay in the property until they find another job, although you need to have an honest conversation with them about whether they can realistically afford to keep renting from you.

6. In debt to payday loan companies

We've all heard stories about people that have borrowed money because they're short at the end of the month and then the loan has quickly spiralled out of control. If the loan company doesn't get paid back in time, they will take money directly from the borrower's bank account. By the time rent is due to be paid to you, your tenant's account may be empty.

7. Partner/sharer moved out

With increasing numbers of families renting a property and divorce rates at around 42% (ONS, Oct 2016), it's possible that the main earner in the household moves out. This is a tricky situation, as it may mean you don't get paid for some time.

You need to check your tenancy agreement and understand legally what you can and can't do under these circumstances. Unfortunately, we still come across cases where we know the local authority is advising tenants to stay in the property until the eviction date, despite the Homeless Act stating that councils should try to rehouse earlier. So you need to get the best legal advice you can, in order to work out how long it will take to evict the tenant and manage your cash flow in the meantime.

8. Illness

If your tenant's ill and unable to work, you may be able to come to an agreement with the tenant where they pay some of the rent due until they're better, then repay you once they go back to work. It may also be possible to secure some benefit help for the tenant.

9. Cut in benefits
Unfortunately, the introduction of benefit caps and problems with Universal Credit payments has led to many people trying to remain in a property they now can't afford. This is a tough situation and you'll need to take legal advice on your short and long-term options.

10. They just want to live in your property rent free!
The most important thing to understand when a tenant doesn't pay their rent is whether they have any intention of doing so. Some tenants make it their business to understand letting laws very well – in many cases, better than their landlords – and are in the habit of not paying rent.

They're often referred to as 'professional bad tenants' (see Chapter 19), who are clever at covering up their past and usually present themselves very well. They will aim to avoid all your communication and will lie and cheat their way through the coming months to live rent-free in your property for as long as possible.

Key steps

When a tenant stops paying their rent:

1. **Contact them right away**
   Call the tenant the day after the rent was due and ask them if there are any problems they're aware of. Work with the tenant, try to speak to them on the phone and remember that eviction should always be a last resort. Make a note to contact them again in seven days.

2. **Check with the bank**
   If the tenant claims to have sent the money, double-check with your

bank whether it's on the way and ask the tenant for proof that the money has left their bank.

3. **Agree a payment plan**
   If the tenant hasn't paid, for any reason, agree how much and by what date(s) they will pay what they owe.

4. **Put it in writing**
   Write to the tenant confirming the payment plan you have agreed and what the next steps will be if the tenant doesn't pay for a second time.

   If your tenant is ignoring you, make a note in your diary to send credit control letters/emails every seven days, demanding your rent. In the third and final demand, you can threaten them with legal possession proceedings.

5. **Seek legal advice**
   If the tenant continues not to pay their rent, you need to speak to a legal specialist to work out the best course of action and decide whether to start eviction proceedings.

Who to work with

The letting agent you work with might be able to help or you can take advice from a specialist legal letting company like ours. You can always contact Landlord Action with any tenant and legal issues and we'll be glad to help you resolve them – call our free advice line on 0333 321 9415.

Questions to ask

Not everyone knows the law when it comes to dealing with tenants, rent arrears and eviction, even if they say they do! Anything to do with lettings is a complex procedure, fraught with legal complications, so make sure you ask any company you're thinking of working with:

1. What are their fees – do you pay by the hour or are they fixed?
2. How long have they been in business?
3. How many evictions do they carry out each year?
4. How many times has the company gone to court to evict a tenant?
5. What are their success rates on resolving tenant issues or getting tenants evicted?

· ·

Hot Tip

ACT QUICKLY. The biggest mistake you can make is accepting a promise from the tenant that they'll pay you today/tomorrow/by the end of the week. You need to address the reason they haven't paid and get the next steps in writing as soon as possible, or you're only going to end up losing money.

· ·

Case Study

Sadly, tenants' circumstances can change and they can lose their job.

All too often, tenants do not advise the landlord of this and can go silent. Some tenants will want to stay in the property as long as possible, because they have nowhere else to go. As a landlord you need to find this out early on, so you can encourage the tenant to apply for benefit and ask for it to be paid direct, if they qualify.

I remember one case, where the tenant lost their job, applied for Housing Benefit but kept the direct payments paid to them and did not pass this on. The debt rose to £13,000, with the landlord having no chance of collecting rent back, because he waited too long to take action.

CHAPTER 37
THE RIGHT WAY TO DEAL WITH TENANTS WHEN THEY DON'T PAY THEIR RENT

Remember, you're not a bank for the tenant!

If a tenant hasn't paid their rent, you may be able to find a way to help them through temporary difficulties so they can stay in the property.

However, most of the time you'll find it's a more serious on-going issue and you need them to leave the property, in which case, you must make sure you evict them in the correct legal way.

It's wise to start eviction proceedings as soon as you realise there's a problem, even if they subsequently repay their arrears and you end up letting them stay. If you aren't covered by your own insurance company, you may have to spend some money on legals (ideally on a fixed-fee basis), but this will be a fraction of the cost of potential loss of rent from a tenant who could also cause significant damage to your property.

Under the Housing Act 1988, there are only two processes that can be used to end an Assured Shorthold Tenancy agreement: Section 21 Notice and Section 8 Notice. There are other eviction processes for different kinds of tenancy, but AST agreements are the most common.

If you have a resident landlord, living and renting within the same property, or the tenant is a company, or if the rent is over £100,000 a year, you would serve a Notice to Quit/forfeiture letter.

There are specific steps you need to take in order to evict a tenant and gain repossession of your property, and the process can take up to two or more months. It's important to understand that if you don't follow the right legal course of action and then end up going to court, your case could be thrown out. Also bear in mind that if you're not successful in court, you may have to pay the tenant's costs. Do try to communicate with the tenant throughout the process, as it may help you to secure the rent you are owed over time.

Differences in Scotland

In Scotland, under a Private Residential Tenancy (see Chapter 5), there are different rules for evicting a tenant for non-payment of rent.

Eviction is mandatory if all of the following apply:

1. The tenant is in arrears of three consecutive months or more
2. The tenant still owes at least one month's rent by the first day of the Tribunal hearing
3. The situation was not due to a delayed or missed payment of a relevant benefit

Eviction is discretionary if the tenant owes less than a month's rent or is no longer in arrears by the first day of the Tribunal hearing. Delays in benefits payments, or other payment problems, will be taken into account in the Tribunal's decision-making.

Key steps

1. **Serve the correct notice**
    Make sure you use the correct Section 8 or Section 21 and that they're served at the right time.

2. **Make sure the tenant has received the notice**
    Either use registered mail or deliver it in person.

3. **Apply to the court, if necessary**
   If the tenant doesn't leave on the notice date, then you apply to the court. In around 60% of cases, tenants leave as soon as a notice is given.

4. **Judicial review**
   The judge reviews the papers submitted. If they are correct and there is no defence, you will be granted possession of the property.

5. **You may continue to pursue the tenant for loss of rent**
   For more information on the process, visit www.landlordaction. co.uk.

Who to work with

It's highly inadvisable to try to handle the eviction process by yourself. If you want your car fixed, you go to a mechanic; if you want to legally evict your tenant you should go to a landlord and tenant specialist firm regulated by the Solicitors Regulation Authority. That's what we do and we do it at a fixed fee so you know exactly how much it's going to cost you.

••

Hot Tip

RECORD EVERYTHING, from the date and time you make phone calls or leave messages to keeping copies of written communication, so if you end up in court, you have the strongest possible case.

CHAPTER 38
DEALING WITH RENT ARREARS WHEN LETTING A ROOM ON A VERBAL AGREEMENT

If you're renting out a room in your own home, you can receive up to £7,500 in rent every year, tax-free! If two of you own the property, this is a joint allowance, you cannot double it. You must pay income tax on anything earned above that amount.

If you're renting a room to a friend or other lodger, you might not have a written tenancy agreement. However, a verbal agreement will exist between you, for example, about how much rent they pay you and when.

You might have agreed they pay some of the household bills or pay for food, while you pay all other costs.

Difficulties are likely to arise if you fall out for any reason and especially if your friend – who is also your tenant – stops paying you the money you'd both agreed on.

If you have no formal, written agreement regarding the situation, you and your tenant are likely to be classed as legally having an 'oral' agreement. This in itself is awkward, as there's very little way for either of you to prove the terms of the original agreement.

Both you and the tenant have some 'implied' rights, which include things such as it being your responsibility to keep the property in a reasonable condition and to provide water and heat, in return for which, the tenant needs to be reasonable and pay you the agreed amount of money/rent on time and in full.

As such, even if you only have an oral agreement, as long as you're keeping up with your responsibilities, you can still take action against your tenant for non-payment of rent.

Key steps

1. **Find out why they're not paying**
   Do they simply not have the money? Has something happened that's out of their control? Will they be able to pay you soon?

2. **Try to find an amicable solution**
   If you find it awkward, perhaps ask a mutual friend to help resolve the situation.

3. **Take expert advice**
   Every situation is different, so don't rely on advice from friends and family – there are plenty of specialists that will give you free advice, including us.

4. **Make sure you're not in the wrong**
   Your tenant could report you to the local authority, so make sure your property is legally up to scratch, just in case.

5. **Put the matter in writing to your friend/lodger**
   Outline how much rent they owe and the date by which they need to pay it, giving them least 14 days. Be sure to keep a copy.

6. **If they don't pay…**
   You have two options: serve them a Section 8 Notice, or Notice to Quit (see Chapter 44) or lock their door and give them their belongings.

7. **If you have served a Section 8 Notice…**
   …and they don't leave, you will need to apply to the courts for possession.

8. **If necessary, hire a bailiff to evict the tenant**
   Remember that you can't use force at any stage and you need to follow the correct legal procedures. We can help with this, so call us on *0333 321 9415.*

Who to work with

In the case of the person being a friend and part of your social group, one of the best people to ask to help you would be a trusted mutual friend.

Otherwise, call Landlord Action, explain your problem and we'll do our best to help you.

Questions to ask

You need to ask your friend/lodger:

1. Why have they stopped paying rent?
2. Do they intend to start paying again?
3. Can they pay any other bills to help around the house?
4. If they can't pay, is there somewhere else they can live?
5. Do they have any relatives, such as mum and dad, that they can ask for help?

If the tenant is your friend and nobody else can help them out, it may be worth offering them some money yourself (if you can afford it) to enable them to leave. This would free up the room so you could re-let it to someone else willing and able to pay.

Hot Tip

HAVE SOMETHING IN WRITING. No matter how close the friend you're letting the room to, always have a written legal agreement, in the form of a licence or, preferably, an AST.

CHAPTER 39
DEALING WITH RENT ARREARS WHEN LETTING A ROOM ON A LICENCE AGREEMENT

A tenancy gives someone a legal right to live in a certain property; a licence simply grants permission to live there.

A licence is typically used when someone is renting a room in your own home, and you're still living in the property. Effectively, it gives the tenant the right to share your accommodation; you are a resident landlord. As their landlord and the owner of the property, you can decide and agree with your tenant what areas of the property they can use and which facilities they can share. For example, if the tenant has an en suite, do they always have to use it, or could they also use the family bathroom?

Letting a room may bring in some extra money, but it can lead to tricky and uncomfortable situations. Bear in mind that when you're not at home, you have no way of knowing which parts of the property your tenant might be using, who's with them and what they're doing, so be careful who you let to and make sure you reference them.

If you are a resident landlord and your relationship with the lodger has broken down, take a step back and make every effort to resolve the matter quickly, don't let it fester. Try not to get emotionally involved, although that can be hard when you're living under the same roof.

If you rent out rooms out in a buy-to-let property that isn't your own home, it will probably be classed as a House in Multiple Occupation and you should use an Assured Shorthold Tenancy. See the next chapter on rent arrears for tenants on ASTs.

It's better to have a licence agreement (also referred to as an excluded tenancy agreement) for a tenant than nothing at all. Even though it doesn't give either you or your tenant as many rights as you have with an AST, it is at least a clear written contract, in addition to which, you both still have basic 'implied rights', as mentioned in the previous chapter.

The big benefit to you of having a licence agreement is that you don't have to go to court to regain possession of the room.

Key steps

1. **Find out why they haven't paid**
   Ask them if there's a problem and try to find an amicable/reasonable solution.

2. **Put the matter in writing to the tenant**
   Outline how much rent they owe, the date by which they need to pay it and what will happen if they fail to pay. Be sure to keep a copy.

3. **Ask them to leave**
   If they don't pay what's owed, give them 'reasonable' notice to quit, such as 14 days or a month, and issue it in writing.

4. **Change the locks**
   If they refuse to leave, you are within your rights to change the locks on their room and the rest of the house, even if their possessions are inside.

5. **Return their possessions to them**
   Note: While you can refuse them entry to the property, you cannot use any force and you cannot hold on to or damage any of their belongings.

Who to work with

It's advisable to contact someone like Citizens Advice for free advice to ensure you don't break the law. Alternatively, you can call the Landlord Action helpline on 0333 321 9415 and we will do our best to help.

Questions to ask

Check with a lettings legal expert:

1. What rights does a licence agreement give you as a landlord?
2. What rights does a licence agreement give the licensee?
3. What do you need to put in writing with regard to arrears?
4. How long should you give the lodger/licensee to make up the arrears?
5. If they don't pay, what can you legally do to regain possession of the room?

....

Hot Tip

ACT QUICKLY. As soon as any lodger, licensee or tenant falls behind with their rent, confirm in writing to them how much is owed and what will happen if they don't pay you by X date.

CHAPTER 40
DEALING WITH RENT ARREARS FOR TENANTS ON AN AST

Your Move found 9.2% of all tenants were behind on their payments in May 2018

If you're letting a whole property to one or more tenants, then you're likely to be doing this via an Assured Shorthold Tenancy agreement (AST), unless you are letting in Scotland where Private Residential Tenancies were introduced in December 2017.

If the tenants are all friends or a group of students, you can issue one AST, where they're all jointly and severally liable; if the tenants are strangers, all moving in and out at different times, you would be better issuing each one with their own AST.

To be able to deal with any rent arrears, you have to make sure your AST is always kept up to date. This includes any updates to the tenancy deposit protection scheme, details of which are typically included in the AST. You and your tenant may need to re-sign the agreement after an update.

If you work with a good letting agent (who is a member of a trade association) on a full management basis, they will ensure the agreement is current. If you're handling the paperwork yourself, work with a legal company to make sure you're always using the latest version of the AST; some online legal document companies will alert you to any updates.

If your agreement is out of date, or you haven't protected the tenant's deposit in a legitimate scheme, you may have problems securing possession of your home, regardless of how far the tenant is in arrears with their rent.

All too often, when a landlord brings us in to help them claim back rent, we find they've used an old version of the AST, which causes massive problems. Not only does it mean you'll struggle to secure the support of the court for rent arrears or securing possession of your property, but any loss of rent insurance you may have may also be rendered invalid.

Remember: if there are arrears, you can serve a Section 8 notice during the fixed term of the tenancy and not have to wait for the fixed period to expire.

Key steps

If your tenant isn't paying their rent, make sure you act quickly – don't just keep your fingers crossed and hope they'll pay up!

1. **Talk to the tenant**
    Call your tenant before you put anything writing to ask what the problem is – it may be a simple error or misunderstanding.

2. **Verify that what they are telling you is correct**

3. **Is it a one-off?**
    Decide whether it's a one-off situation or whether the tenant is likely to keep falling behind.

4. **Come to an agreement**
    Agree with the tenant how much will be paid and by when, and confirm it in writing. Always give the tenant a chance to pay – we can all fall on hard times. You may want to do a deal with your tenant and possibly write off the rent arrears if they give you vacant possession. If that happens you need them to sign a Deed of Surrender

5. **Serve the appropriate Notice**
    If the tenant doesn't make good the rent arrears, serve them with either a Section 21 or Section 8 Notice (see Chapters 43 and 44).

6. **Go to court**

   If the tenant refuses to leave, you may need to go to court to secure possession.

7. **Engage a bailiff**

   Make sure the eviction is carried out legally by a bailiff, who may be court appointed.

8. **Pursue the tenant for arrears**

   After they've been evicted, you should be able to continue to pursue the tenant for arrears, if you think it's worthwhile.

Who to work with

Always seek professional advice before you take any action, either from a legal company, an organisation such as Citizen's Advice, or contact us at Landlord Action.

And if you have specialist landlord insurance to cover you for lost rent, check with them what to do to chase any arrears. If you haven't adhered to their guidelines or processes, they may not pay up.

There are lots of companies out there who promise to help you with problem tenants, but before you engage them:

1. Check whether they're authorised to work on behalf of mortgage and insurance companies.

2. Ask if they offer a fixed-fee service for securing rent arrears or evicting a tenant, if required.

3. Confirm they have experience and a good track record of securing rent arrears.

4. Make sure the company is regulated by the Solicitors Regulation Authority which means it has to abide by the rules of the Law Society. It is imperative a solicitor is on record because if there is a problem at court you want a landlord and tenant specialist acting for you. Beware: there are a lot of unregulated eviction companies which do not use solicitors

5. Make sure they have professional indemnity Insurance in place.

6. Make sure the solicitors you use have a good reputation in landlord and tenant law.

Questions to ask

If you have insurance to cover rent arrears, you need to check with your insurance company:

1. What evidence they need to be able to repay you lost rent.
2. Whether there's an excess on the policy, for example, one month's rent.
3. What length of time rent will be paid for.
4. Whether they'll cover any legal fees.
5. If there are any specific companies you need to use to help you recover lost rent.
6. Always read their terms and conditions.

Hot Tip

GET EXPERT ADVICE BEFORE YOU ACT. If you've already started eviction proceedings, or gone to court by the time you contact us at Landlord Action, we won't be able to give you any free help because we'll have to engage a solicitor. Contact us as soon as there is a problem and we can give you expert advice at no cost. Call 0333 363 5458 or complete the contact form at www.landlordaction.co.uk/contact.

CHAPTER 41
DEALING WITH RENT ARREARS FOR TENANTS RECEIVING HOUSING BENEFIT/UNIVERSAL CREDIT

Over the last few years, the government has been rolling out a new scheme called Universal Credit, which will have reached every area in Great Britain by the end of 2018, and replace all existing means-tested benefits by 2022/3.

The scheme pays all benefits to tenants on a monthly basis and then requires the tenants to pay their rent from this to the landlord, prompting concerns that landlords are going to be owed more rent arrears; an issue I highlighted on BBC1's The One Show in May 2013.

I understood the ideas and reasoning behind the government wanting to bring in Universal Credit in theory… but unfortunately the practicality so far has not worked.

Landlords need to feel secure that they will receive their rent, so I believe it should be paid directly to them by the scheme. Instead, they have to wait for there to be a problem with arrears before they can apply for direct payments from their tenants.

Local authorities are strongly promoting social tenants to private landlords but, although more properties are needed for those on benefits, many landlords are now pulling out of this sector.

A National Landlords Association survey in 2017 found that just two in 10 landlords say they would consider letting to tenants on Housing Benefit or Universal Credit. This is backed up by the feedback we are getting from landlords; many want to exit the housing benefit market as they are worried about receiving their rent arrears because they are not receiving direct payments from councils. As a result, we have had to take court action and possession.

The Homelessness Reduction Act 2017, which came into force in April 2018, compels local authorities to rehouse a tenant within 56 days of being told they have received an eviction notification. They face huge challenges in rehousing them due to the great shortages of local authority housing and the already long waiting lists for housing; latest government figures (March 2017) showed that there were 1.16million households on waiting lists for council properties.

In addition, the benefit caps have meant many tenants and landlords are now finding it difficult – even impossible – to make ends meet. Some landlords are having to evict tenants on benefits because the tenant can't afford to make up the rent owed and the only way the landlord is able to cover their costs is by renting to someone who can pay the rent themselves.

And, in many cases, landlords can't rent to people on benefits because their mortgage company doesn't allow it and/or they struggle to secure insurance.

It is widely reported that tenants on housing benefits will generally stay in a property longer and look after it better – in fact, I have come across many landlords who only rent to housing benefit tenants and their portfolios work really well – but, for many landlords, the risks outweigh the benefits. Of course, much depends on where your property is and what type of tenants you can attract.

Just beware that advertising 'no DSS' or 'no benefits' could be seen as discrimination. For more information, see Chapter 16.

Risks and rewards of renting to tenants on benefits
*   In some cases, the local authority's housing team may organise for the rent to be paid directly to you, although the deposit may or may not be paid in full. If you don't receive a deposit, the local authority will often guarantee the amount for you, should a claim be made.

- In other cases, the local authority (LA) may guarantee the rent to you now, but not in the future – or they may not give you any guarantees at all.
- If the local authority likes your property, with such huge waiting lists, it's likely they'll always be able to find you a tenant very quickly, which could mean no voids and not having to incur the cost of re-letting the property, as you would in the private sector.
- When renting to recipients of Housing Benefit, if the tenant falls into rent arrears, you can turn to the local authority for help. There is a similar system under Universal Credit; if the tenant owes at least two months' rent, you can apply for a "managed payment" – where the rent is paid directly to you – by completing a form which can be found on the government website. DWP may decide to offer budgeting support to the tenant instead. And if the tenant can prove they are not in arrears – or that they are in dispute with you – they may challenge your application and your request may be refused.

I should say at this point, that most LHA tenants do actually pay their rent on time and in full! As with so many areas of buy-to-let, it's the few bad ones who tend to tarnish a whole group of people.

In terms of pursuing the tenant personally for arrears, unfortunately the reality of the situation is that if they're on LHA or Universal Credit there's probably very little money available for you to claim back. The best thing to do is simply regain possession of your property as soon as possible.

Key steps

1. Speak to the tenant
Ask your tenant why they're not paying their rent – find out whether they're waiting for a payment themselves, or if they're simply not managing their money properly.

2. **If your tenant is receiving Housing Benefit (LHA), speak to the local authority**

   Call the local authority, then put in writing what rent arrears the tenant owes. Ideally, set up a meeting with the local authority to see whether you can get the rent paid to you directly. In some cases, the local authority may be able to use additional funds to keep the tenant in the property.

3. **If your tenant is receiving Universal Credit, apply for a managed payment**

   When a tenant is two months or more in arrears, you can download a form from the government website and apply for the tenant's housing portion of their Universal Credit to be paid directly to you. This is called a "managed payment" or "alternative payment arrangement". Your application will be discussed with the tenant and considered on a case by case basis. You will be advised of DWP's decision but, if the application is refused, you will not be told why, for data protection reasons.

4. **Evict the tenant**

   If the arrears situation cannot be resolved, you will have to begin eviction proceedings, as outlined in the previous chapter. Always talk to the local authority/DWP before you take any action against a tenant – especially if they've lived in and looked after your property for a long time.

Who to work with

The best place to go for help, and certainly your first port of call, is your local authority. You may be able to do this best via your local landlord association, especially if it's part of a local authority accreditation scheme.

If you don't have any joy with your LA, speak to your insurance company to see what the next steps are, then you may need to engage a rent arrears specialist.

Questions to ask

Before you rent to a tenant on benefits, ask the local authority:

1. What schemes do they have for private landlords to rent to tenants receiving LHA or Universal Credit?
2. Are these schemes expected to be in place for months or years?
3. Will they pay rent directly to you now and in the future?
4. Do they take care of everything you need to rent the property legally, eg protect any deposit, provide an Energy Performance Certificate or inventory?
5. What will they do if there are problems with the tenant, eg falling into arrears with the rent?

If the tenant is going to be paying you rent themselves, check with them that they will:

1. Use some form of automatic payment, such as via a bank account or credit union.
2. Pass normal credit checks.
3. Have submitted their benefit claim forms (ideally do this with them).
4. Give you a copy of confirmation of their benefits.
5. Understand what happens if they don't pay rent to you.

••

Hot Tip

CHOOSE LANDLORD-FRIENDLY LOCAL AUTHORITIES. Only rent to tenants on benefits if their local authority works proactively with private landlords, eg they run schemes to find and fund tenants and/or have landlord accreditation schemes.

The law protects tenants from being homeless, and it protects landlords' property rights too.

We affect people's lives, so we make sure we do things right... first time.

Fixed-fee eviction services have been the bread & butter of our offering since 1999. As well as tenant eviction our solicitors also specialise in drafting legal documents, general landlord-tenant matters and debt recovery. As part of the Hamilton Fraser family, access to expert staff and enhanced systems means there's never any danger of us spreading ourselves too thinly.

LANDLORD ACTION

0333 321 9415
landlordaction.co.uk

CHAPTER 42
CHOOSING AN EVICTION COMPANY

In 1999 I started Landlord Action with Johnathan Chippeck and, in doing so, the fixed fee eviction industry, because I thought solicitors were charging landlords too much money.

If you search for 'evicting a tenant' on Google, there are more than 310,000 results but, as with any service, not all eviction companies are the same.

Many eviction specialists now offer fixed fees, as do some legal companies; others charge by the hour. Some will offer cheap fees and I'm afraid you'll get a cheap service from people who aren't experts. At the same time, we believe you shouldn't have to pay huge fees based on hourly rates.

While writing the first edition of this book, we became regulated by the Solicitors Regulation Authority, so now we employ solicitors and paralegals to carry out the legal work in-house. Having this level of expertise at hand makes a big difference to the speed at which we can respond to matters and deal with a case.

These are the three biggest mistakes we see amateur companies making:

1. **Compliance errors**
   We often take over cases that have been thrown out of court because the original eviction company hasn't filed the right notice.

2. **Attempting shortcuts**
   Some companies make shortcuts in an effort to try to save money. For example, they often just complete the forms and ask the landlord to sign, then expect the landlords to carry out the hearings themselves. It's imperative that solicitors are named on the court record. If not, ask the company why they are not using solicitors to be instructed.

3. **Taking a 'standard' course of action**

   Some companies simply don't take enough time to find out and understand the specific details of your case. While the eviction process is, for the most part, a set course of action, if they've overlooked something and not appreciated exactly what's taken place between you and the tenant, when the case goes to court the tenant could easily find a reason to argue that the action isn't legal.

Key steps

To find the right eviction company for you, you need to understand the critical steps of the eviction process. When you speak to them, make sure you go through these points:

1. **Be completely honest**

   Have an open and honest discussion about all the problems between you and the tenant.

2. **Give the whole picture**

   Don't just tell the eviction company the things the tenant has done wrong, such as not paying rent or causing damage to the property. Have your records about their whole tenancy to hand. Have they asked for repairs which you haven't carried out?

3. **Check their recommendation**

   Be sure that the notice the eviction company suggests you serve is the correct one (see chapters on Section 8 and Section 21).

4. **How quickly do they serve?**

   Ask them how quickly they serve the notice; it should be within 48 hours.

5. **Are they regulated by the Solicitors Regulation Authority?**

6. **Find out who they use to serve notices.**

7. **How do they confirm notices have been served?**

8. **Next steps...**
   If the tenant doesn't respond to the notice, will the eviction company then commence court proceedings?

9. **Does the price include legal representation in court?**

10. **Check whether you need to be in court.**

11. **What if they do something wrong?**
    What happens to the money you've paid if it turns out the company has served the wrong notices?

Who to work with

You should work with a company that:

1. Has at least five years' tenancy eviction experience.

2. Asks to see your tenancy agreement.

3. Queries all of the issues between you and the tenant.

4. Uses their own qualified paralegals and solicitors.

5. Charges fixed fees.

6. Do some research on the company: who recommends them and how many employees do they have?

Landlord Action has carried out more than 35,000 instructions, which means we have a great deal of experience in:

1. Different eviction process for different tenancy agreements.

2. Helping landlords evict tenants without any legal proceedings.

3. Serving the correct notices.

4. Facilitating 60% of tenant evictions purely through serving the right notice.

5. Completing legal paperwork.

6. Dealing with court cases on your behalf.

7. Following up the eviction with bailiffs.

8. Securing the property back for you.

9. Knowing the importance of in-house legal services, rather than outsourcing.

10. Charging fair fixed fees, which we know will cover everything, from serving notices through to carrying out the eviction.

There are other companies out there who will also do a good job on evictions. The important thing is to shop around to find the best service, not the cheapest deal.

Questions to ask

Here are the questions you should ask an eviction company, together with our own answers, to give you an idea of what responses you should look for:

1. **Do you use regulated solicitors to issue the possession proceedings?**

   If they say no, it's advisable to find to a company which uses or is regulated by the Solicitors Regular Authority as it gives you somewhere to go if you want to file a complaint. Also if they are not regulated, they are not allowed to put their names on the court record; it can only be in the landlord's name or a firm regulated by the SRA.

2. **Do you have valid Professional Indemnity Insurance to carry out Landlord and Tenant possession cases?**

   Ask to see if this and if they refuse, do not use them, as you will not be covered for any losses, if they have acted negligently in an instruction.

3. **Can you provide me with testimonials from satisfied customers?**

   This will give you a peace of mind when instructing.

4. **Finally, ask them whether they have received any awards for their eviction services – and check up on what they say!**

Hot Tip

ALWAYS TRY TO AVOID LEGAL ACTION. Our quickest tenant vacation to date is two days following the serving of a notice. However, that's unusual!

If a tenant doesn't want to vacate, it could take you up to five months to get your property back – that's five months of legal fees and mortgage payments to make, without any rent coming in. Do all you can to resolve a dispute so that the tenant leaves of their own accord and you can get another tenant in as soon as possible – one who'll pay the rent!

Case Study

A recent county court appeal – Kassam v Gill & Gill – drew attention to the problems of using unregulated 'eviction specialists'. The landlords had appointed an unregulated company called Remove a Tenant, part of Fentham Group Ltd, to serve a Section 8 Notice on their tenant. Unfortunately they made errors which rendered it invalid.

In addition, the judge ruled that some of the services offered by Remove a Tenant – eg completing the possession claim forms on the landlord's behalf – breached the terms of the Legal Services Act 2007, due to their unregulated status. This could spell the end for unregulated eviction specialists as, to remain within the law, there are very few services they can offer. This is definitely a case where cheap turned out to be expensive.

CHAPTER 43
SECTION 21 NOTICE

To ensure you are able to serve a Section 21 Notice, it is important to set up the tenancy correctly in the first place, ensuring you protect the deposit and serve the prescribed information at the right time.

We pick things up when they go wrong and we see many incorrect Section 21 notices served by landlords and letting agents that have to be served again. A lot of the time tenants will vacate a property on these notices, not knowing that they are incorrect and they could legally ignore them.

Tenants now are more educated and of course can obtain more legal advice from organisations such as Shelter and Citizens Advice so it is even more important to get it right first time.

All tenancies now come under the Deregulation Act, regardless of start date, so you will have had to have served the prescribed information (See Chapters 10 and 21) and follow the rules which apply. Since 1st October 2018, the Section 21 6a Notice is now the only applicable Section 21 Notice that can be served.

- If you fail to provide the prescribed information and protect the tenant's deposit, you will not be able to issue a Section 21 6a notice to regain possession of your property. If a property is an HMO and you do not have the correct licence, you can't serve a Section 21 6a Notice.
- In a move to end 'retaliatory evictions', if you fail to respond to a tenant's written request for repairs within 14 days, the tenant could escalate this complaint to the local authority. If the repairs are deemed 'very serious', the local authority could enforce and serve an improvement or hazardous notice on the landlord, preventing you from serving Section 21 notice for six months.

- In the past, a Section 21 notice could be served at the start of a tenancy; now it cannot be served within the first four months of the contractual term of the tenancy. This is to stop the bad practice of landlords and their agents serving notice at the start of a tenancy to enable them to finish it at their convenience.
- If a Section 21 6a has been served, it has to be acted on within six months, so use it or lose it. In the past there was no deadline and at Landlord Action we have been instructed to act on Section 21 notices which have been four years old, which just isn't fair.
- Section 21 prescribed 6a forms form are more straightforward and the claims process is simplified as it doesn't request the complicated end-dates previously required with periodic tenancies; these were often used to reject possession claims due to errors with dates.

Why serve a Section 21 notice?

A Section 21 Notice explains to a tenant that the landlord wants the property back, without having to give any reasons. It can only be given to tenants on agreements with a fixed term (six or 12 months) that has expired. Typically this applies to tenants on ASTs.

The majority of the time landlords serve a Section 21 notice is for one of these reasons:

- they are looking to sell their property (especially with the impending Section 24 tax changes)
- they wish to move into the property because their personal circumstances have changed
- because tenants are still being told to stay in the property so they don't make themselves voluntarily homeless and can look to be rehoused by the local authority
- rent arrears.

In the case of rent arrears, a Section 8 notice can be served (see Chapter 44) but this can be a longer process, often resulting in no collection of rent arrears, so landlords are tending to serve a Section 21 notice instead, writing off the rent which there is little chance of collecting, and resulting in a simpler procedure.

I explained all this recently on BBC Panorama when the words 'non-fault' were used but let's be clear: landlords are using Section 21 because there is a reason and, often, because there is a fault.

One of the benefits to you of serving a Section 21 Notice, rather than a Section 8 is you do not have to give a reason why you want the property back. Because you have to give the tenant two months' notice, it also means they have plenty of time to find somewhere else to live and there's less likely to be any hard feelings. In my experience, the more notice you give a tenant to quit the property, the more likely they are to move out on time.

However, Section 21 Notices are no longer as easy a solution to regain possession as they once were! Only an experienced eviction company (or legal practice) that has taken the time to understand all the different issues between you and the tenant can work out which notice it would be better to serve.

The reasons to serve a Section 21 Notice are:

1. You want to move back in (it might have been your home).

2. You have a new tenant you'd like to move into the property (it might be a member of the family or someone you know).

3. Your tenant has stopped paying rent, but you only have two months left to go before the end of their fixed-term tenancy agreement.

4. The tenant has moved someone else into the property without your permission.

5. You haven't maintained the property as well as you should.

6. Tenants are requesting a Section 21 notice to be served so they can try to be rehoused by the local authority.

Do NOT serve a Section 21 Notice if you haven't provided the legally required prescribed information to the tenant within 30 days (or don't have evidence you have) or if you haven't protected your tenant's deposit in one of the government's schemes (see Chapter 25), otherwise the tenant could make a claim against you. They could end up staying in the property and you may even have to pay compensation of up to three times the deposit as you have broken the law.

The effect of housing benefit caps

Following the introduction of housing benefit caps, many more evictions are taking place, as tenants can't afford to make up the shortfall in rent and are falling into arrears. As a result, the system has been put under pressure, as local authorities struggle to re-house social tenants, due to a lack of social housing. Although the Homelessness Reduction Act means local authorities are obliged to rehome anyone who is threatened with homelessness within 56 days, in reality, the severe shortage of housing means there is nowhere to put them. This has resulted in a push-back by local councils, who are still advising tenants to stay put until the bailiffs turn up to evict them. This buys the council some time as will be about four-six months before the eviction takes place.

Essentially, the local council will no longer accept a Section 21 Notice alone as proof that the tenant is no longer going to be living at your property; they require a court order for possession and a date for eviction by a bailiff. Some tenants are therefore unlikely to take much notice of you serving them with a Section 21 Notice – they'll simply stay in the property until you pay to take them through the courts.

The pressure of increasing numbers of evictions has also meant judges are now particularly keen to ensure the paperwork is 100% accurate before they grant a possession that could make someone homeless. The slightest error on your part – or on the part of the company handling your eviction – and the judge is likely to throw the judgment out.

If you don't rent to tenants on benefits, you might think you don't need to worry about this, but you'd be wrong. This kind of information travels very quickly around tenants and the organisations and charities that advise them, so more and more tenants are becoming aware that they can stay in a property – potentially rent free – if they ignore the Section 21 Notice and wait to hear from a court and bailiff.

Importantly, if you're going to issue a Section 21 Notice, you must be completely honest about everything that's happened and make sure you've complied with all your legal responsibilities and obligations as a landlord. For example, did you provide the correct prescribed information, are your safety certificates up to date and have you protected the tenant's deposit correctly?

Key steps to issuing a Section 21 Notice (England and Wales)

Issuing the notice isn't complicated; doing it right is. You must make sure it is 100% correct so that if you end up in court, they grant you with possession without question.

1. **Is it the right notice?**
   Make sure the Section 21 Notice is the fastest way to evict your tenant.

2. **Find out how long it'll take**
   Check with local legal companies how long you'll have to wait for a court order.

3. **Check when the tenant's fixed term comes to an end**

4. **Fixed term or periodic?**

5. **Be clear whether you're serving the notice to fall exactly at the end of the fixed term or when the tenancy has become periodic**

6. **Make sure dates are correct for a periodic tenancy**
   If you're serving an old Section 21 Notice under a periodic tenancy (tenancies renewed before 1st October 2015), the notice must be served on the last day of the period, ie the day before the next rent payment is due.

7. **Give the correct notice period**
   Make sure you give the tenant two months' notice to leave.

8. **Factor in the time to deliver the notice**
   If you're posting the notice, allow some extra days to account for the time it'll take to arrive with the tenant.

9. **Confirm receipt**
   Make sure you have evidence that the tenant has received the notice and on what day. Use recorded delivery or have an eviction specialist serve the notice in person.

10. **If the tenant doesn't leave, you'll have to apply to the court for a possession order**

11. **Instruct a bailiff, if necessary**
    If the court grants possession and the tenant still doesn't move out, you'll need to use a bailiff to evict the tenant legally.

Who to work with

You can download Section 21 6a Notices from the government website (www.gov.uk/guidance/assured-tenancy-forms) for free, although I'd advise against completing and serving one yourself as it could result in unnecessary delays. First, you have to choose the right Section 21 Notice and, secondly, if a court later decides you've done something wrong, you'll have to start the process again from scratch and will have wasted two months or more, in both time and lost rent.

If you are unsure, let one of my qualified legal team help you with this, so you get it right first time. Getting it wrong can cost you.

Questions to ask

The key questions you need to ask yourself are about the issues with your tenant, and you'll need to give answers to the following questions to whoever's dealing with your eviction case:

1. Why do you want the tenant out of the property?
2. Has the tenant made any complaints about you?
3. Have they put any of these complaints in writing?
4. What are they claiming you have done?
5. Is there any merit in their claims?
6. Have you answered any of their complaints, either verbally or in writing?
7. Have you rectified anything they've raised?
8. Has the tenant done anything that breaches the tenancy agreement?
9. List all the things they have done to breach their agreement
10. What evidence do you have of what they've done?

Scotland

Tenancies work differently in Scotland. If the tenancy began or was renewed after 1st December 2017, it will be a private residential tenancy. These tenancies are open-ended, so you cannot impose a fixed term or ask a tenant to leave just because the initial six-month period is up.

Under a private residential tenancy, if the tenant has been in the property for six months or more, you will need to give them at least 84 days' notice to leave, unless they have broken the terms of the agreement.

For assured tenancies in Scotland (begun or renewed before 1st December 2017) you have to give at least 40 days' notice to quit, if the tenant has lived in the property for more than four months.

For more information about serving notices in Scotland, visit www.rentingscotland.org/landlords/ending-the-tenancy

●●●

Hot Tip

Note: Since writing this book, the government has entered into consultation about the use of Section 21 Notices. There is talk of giving tenants three months' notice instead of two, and that a landlord moving back into their property, selling or cases of rent arrears will not be able to be used as grounds for a Section 21 Notice. Instead, these will become additional grounds for a Section 8 Notice. So watch this space.

CHAPTER 44
SECTION 8 NOTICE

71% of landlords take eviction action because of rent arrears.
(Source: Landlord Action)

A Section 8 Notice allows landlords to secure possession of their property on various grounds, as laid out in Schedule 2 of the Housing Act 1988. The grounds have been updated in the past few years so make sure you use the latest Notices.

There are 17 grounds for eviction, of two types; mandatory, where the tenant will certainly be ordered to leave, and discretionary, where the court can decide one way or the other, depending on what can be proven.

From our perspective, we need to be confident that we can prove the tenant's breach of tenancy under at least one of the mandatory grounds. If we can, the court is compelled to grant your possession.

The mandatory grounds on which a Section 8 Notice can be issued include:

Ground 2
This is typically used by lenders who want to repossess the property and need the tenant to leave before they can sell it.

During the recession, many lenders have chosen to continue to rent out landlords' properties, even though the landlord isn't paying the mortgage, as the rental income has often covered the arrears. Some landlords have even gained their property back as they become able once again to cover all the costs. In other cases, the lenders will continue to rent the property out until prices recover enough for them to sell, reducing the liability for the landlord.

Ground 7b

This is a new mandatory ground for possession, introduced with the Immigration Act 2016, and can be used if any of the occupants are believed to have no Right to Rent in the UK. The Home Office may inform you that your tenant is renting illegally, by sending you a Notice of Letting to a Disqualified Person. When you have acted on this notice, you must let the Home Office know.

There are several other options open to you if you discover one or more of your tenants have no Right to Rent in the UK. These are listed on the government website: www.gov.uk/guidance/ending-a-tenancy-due-to-immigration-status

Ground 8

This is to do with rent arrears and is the most common reason for a Section 8 Notice to be issued. The tenant must be two months behind if they pay monthly, and eight weeks behind if they pay weekly.

Some example discretionary grounds are:

Ground 10

A landlord can request the property back because of a situation arising from rent arrears that are less than those covered in Ground 8. It might be you owe the mortgage lender money or are now in financial hardship as a result of the tenant not paying you rent.

Ground 15

If you've let your property furnished, you can use this ground to recover the property if the tenant – or their visitors – have caused damage to your belongings. You'll need to produce evidence, such as an inventory with pictures and written descriptions of 'before' and 'after'.

Ground 17

If you discover that the tenant has not been honest with information they supplied in their application, you can ask for the property back on this ground. For example, the tenant may have given a false identity or false references, or they might have lied about how much they earned and can't now afford the on-going rental payments.

It's important you consider which notice is best to serve: 21 or 8. If there are large rent arrears and the tenant has means to pay or there is a guarantor, Section 8 is usually a good choice, as it can help reduce your financial losses. And if, for any reason, you haven't complied fully with the deposit scheme legislation, then it's better to serve a Section 8 rather than a Section 21 Notice. Other times it's better to serve a Section 8 Notice include:

1. When the tenant is on a fixed-term agreement and there are more than two months to go until it ends.

2. If the tenant is still paying rent, but clearly not looking after your property.

3. If the tenant is still paying rent, but is causing a nuisance to neighbours.

4. If you find out the tenant isn't who they say they are.

However, there are some downsides:

1. If you're owed money, the court can grant you a money order against the tenant, but you'll have to still pursue the tenant for money yourself, which may cost you more than the tenant owes.

2. The tenant can defend themselves against you and secure free help from various organisations and charities.

3. If you lose the court case, the tenant could be awarded legal costs against you.

4. Or the judge may grant a suspended possession order, where you have to rely on the tenant to default on a rent payment before you can apply for an eviction date.

And, if you're based in London, it can take six weeks or longer to get a court date!

Key steps

To issue a Section 8 Notice, you need to be confident that:

1. **You have more than one ground on which to issue the Notice**

2. **One of the grounds is mandatory (ideally)**

3. **The tenant has no defence**
   There's nothing the tenant can use as substantial defence against your claim for possession.

Once you're clear on the grounds, you need to:

4. **Give the right dates for the notice to be served**
   Double-check dates for periodic tenancies, which will depend on the frequency of rental payments.

5. **Fill in the form correctly**

6. **Serve the notice to the tenant**

7. **Have evidence they have received the notice**
   Send via recorded mail or deliver in person

8. **Be prepared for the cost of going to court**

Who to work with

Issuing a Section 8 Notice can be complicated – there are 17 different grounds you could issue it on and you have to be careful you're not adding grounds out of anger and frustration with the tenant. If you can't prove all the grounds in court, you could waste a lot of time and money and still not get your property back.

That's why it's best to work with an eviction specialist who can act objectively on your behalf. Calmly taking the correct legal course of action, in a professional manner, lets the tenant know you're serious. That's why 60% of tenants in the cases we deal with leave after we've issued them notices, without the need for any further action, saving you time and money.

We serve dozens of notices on a weekly basis and we have a team of process servers nationwide hand-delivering Section 8 Notices at the property. We often hand-deliver them very early in the morning to try to catch the tenant in (and preferably get them out of bed!) so that it makes an impact and so that the landlord will hopefully receive his rent arrears if not his property at this earlier stage. And of course a witness statement is provided to the court if necessary.

Questions to ask

1. Which of the grounds for eviction do you have strong evidence for, that you are confident would stand up in court?
2. Of these grounds, are you going to use all of them, or just the minimum required?
3. Are there any counter-claims the tenant could make that could cause problems for you in court?

Hot Tip

GET IT RIGHT FIRST TIME. Choose grounds you can prove and serve the Section 8 Notice correctly first time, to give yourself the best chance, should it end up in court. Make sure you use the updated forms, introduced in December 2016.

Case Study

Our legal team sends out numerous Section 8 Notices on a daily basis for landlords and letting agents across England and Wales, mainly for rent arrears.

The other main ground for Section 8 breach of tenancy has been subletting, as a result of rising rents and the need for shared accommodation. Some tenants are blatantly breaching tenancy agreements and subletting rooms to try to maximise income, especially when uploading and advertising the properties on holiday websites such as Airbnb.

On one case where we served a Section 8 notice for subletting, we had a tenant we believe was making between £4,000 and £5,000 a month, advertising the property as a boutique-style property in Chiswick. People were coming and going all the time, causing the landlord no end of stress, financially and emotionally.

CHAPTER 45
GOING TO THE SMALL CLAIMS COURT

You can now claim up to £10,000 of debt from the Small Claims Court.

The Small Claims Court (SCC) in England and Wales is a very useful system for both landlords and tenants, as it's a fairly straightforward process and relatively inexpensive.

From your perspective, the SCC can be a cost-effective way to make a claim against your tenant for rent arrears and/or damage to your property.

There's a claim limit of £10,000 but, even if the tenant owes you more, as the legal costs are likely to be zero or much lower than a full court, you might still come out ahead in net terms.

On average, it costs somewhere between £25 and £350 to go to the SCC, depending on how much you're claiming from the tenant. You can add loss of earnings and any legal fees associated with the claim too.

In my experience, a key benefit of the SCC is it's much less stressful than regular courts – it's more like having a meeting at work and there's a lot less legal jargon.

However, you should bear in mind that, just like the court system, there's no guarantee you'll be able to secure your money from the tenant, even if you win. The court can only confirm you're owed the money and guide you to different methods of collecting what is now a 'debt'. In short, these are the ways you can claim the money owed:

- A bailiff can collect the money or goods to the value of the debt
- Deductions can be made directly from the tenant's wages, if they're employed
- The tenant's bank account can be frozen until the debt is paid
- A charge can be placed on the tenant's home/land/other property owned, so it can't be sold unless you receive the money owed.

These methods can work if the tenant has a job or money, goods or property to the value of the debt. However if they don't, I'm afraid there's little point pursuing them. The only benefit would be knowing that the tenant now had a County Court Judgment (CCJ) against them, which would make it tough for them to secure another property or finance in the future. (See the next chapter: Going to court.) Any court, even small claims, would prefer you try to settle disputes, so make sure you have proof you've tried to resolve the issue with the tenant and that you have clear evidence of what the tenant owes you.

If you are a business and you are trying to pursue debt from a tenant, you will need to a send a Letter of Claim to the tenant, including the following information:

- Up-to-date statement of account, including any interest or other charges
- The date the tenancy began/was renewed and where and where the agreement was signed
- If the tenant has offered to pay in instalments, or has been doing so, and this is unacceptable, explain why
- Details of how the debt can be paid, such as payment methods and address for payment
- Contact details if the tenant wishes to discuss the debt
- Information Sheet, Reply Form and Financial Statement Form, all available at www.justice.gov.uk/courts/procedure-rules/civil/pdf/protocols/debt-pap.pdf
- Address where their reply should be sent.

To start the claim against the tenant you need to file it at Money Claim Online (moneyclaim.gov.uk). If you get stuck, there's a helpline and there are also people at the SCC who can advise on all the steps you need to take, but bear in mind they won't give you any legal advice.

Once you've filled in a questionnaire about your claim, a district judge will decide whether it can be heard in the SCC and it will be allocated by the court as a 'small' (claims under £10,000), 'fast' (claims over £10,000) or 'multi-track' (claims over £25,000 or for complex points of law) case. If it's considered 'fast' or 'multi-track', the advice from the courts is to consult a legal adviser, such as Landlord Action.

(If your property is in Scotland, it's a similar system, but with a few differences – visit scotcourts.gov.uk for more information.)

Key steps

Although the Small Claims Court is more straightforward than regular court, there are still various steps you need to take and lots of different types of forms to complete, depending on the nature of your case. That's why it's worth seeking either free or paid-for advice to make sure you get the process right from the start.

1. **Have the tenant's details**
   Make sure you have the tenant's full name, current address and phone number.

2. **Can they pay you?**
   Before you take any action, check that the tenant has the ability to pay you some or all of the money, ie that it's going to be worthwhile.

3. **Do your research**
   Make sure you read the information on the Government's website www.gov.uk/make-court-claim-for-money about making a claim via the Small Claims Court and understand exactly what's involved.

4. **Try to resolve the issue**

Do what you can to solve the dispute before starting the claims process. Write to the tenant, allow them to make a smaller payment than they owe, stage payments, or accept goods to the value of the money they owe you. Make sure you keep all correspondence and record any conversations you've had.

5. **Give the tenant notice you intend to take action**

If you're unable to resolve the dispute, then send a 'letter before action', giving the tenant 14 days to pay, prior to you starting court proceedings.

6. **Gather evidence**

Pull together evidence of non-payment of rent or money the tenant owes you for damages – things such as:

   a. The tenancy agreement
   b. An inventory, showing 'before' and 'after'
   c. Bank statements
   d. Letters sent requesting payment
   e. Any responses from the tenant
   f. Evidence you have tried to settle fairly with the tenant
   g. Any witnesses (eg neighbours)
   h. Receipts to prove ownership of damaged property.

7. **Put forward your claim online**

If the tenant/debtor fails to file a reply or defence within 28 days, then you can apply for a money judgment in default.

8. **Receive the District Judge's decision**

Your claim will be allocated as small, fast or multi-tracked. Seek legal advice if the judge declares you have a fast or multi-tracked claim. There are different forms to complete for each: N194A for small; N149B for fast track; N194C for multi-track.

9. **Arrange a date to go to the Small Claims Court**

From a time perspective, a small claim that isn't defended could take as little as six weeks, while a more complex case could take six months to a year to be concluded.

Who to work with

You can do all the small claims work yourself. Even if the claim is fast or multi-tracked, you can still do all the work, you'll just need proper legal help and advice along the way. At Landlord Action, we can do all of this for you, but it does take time. To begin with, we would make sure the 'pre-action' you have to prove to the court is carried out first, including finding the tenant and establishing whether it's worth pursuing them through the SCC in the first place.

Once the pre-action is done, we can carry out the online money claim for you and organise to pay the court fee.

For more information, visit our website: www.landlordaction.co.uk/debt-recovery/residential-debt-recovery/

Questions to ask

You need to decide whether you can do all the work yourself, need a little legal help, or want to hand over the whole case to a legal company to handle it on your behalf.

To help with this decision you need to work out:

1. What forms you need to fill in.
2. Whether you have all the information you need to complete the forms.
3. How much time the process will take.

4. Whether you'll be able to take time off work to attend court.
5. If the tenant defends the case, can you counteract their claims?
6. Whether you're comfortable with putting forward your own case and defending yourself against anything the tenant may accuse you of?

While you might feel confident in your abilities when you're sat at home, the reality of a court environment can have quite an effect. Unless you're experienced in giving presentations and speaking in public, I'd recommend you secure the help of a legal professional who's experienced in such cases – and has a track record of winning!

••

Hot Tip

MAKE SURE IT'S WORTHWHILE. Make sure the tenant can pay some, if not all of the debt **before** you take any legal action.

CHAPTER 46
GOING TO COURT

In 2017 there were more than 132,000 possession claims issued in England and Wales. (Source: Ministry of Justice figures)

Over the last few years, I've seen a sharp rise not only in the number of cases for rent arrears, but also in the number of tenants defending themselves against landlords in court.

The knock-on effect is that the court process for landlords to regain possession of their property is getting longer and longer. If a court date is set, the tenant then puts in a defence and the case is adjourned, it's effectively created two cases from one. The more cases there are in the system, the longer it takes to get a court date and the longer the tenant can stay in your property, potentially without paying rent.

We act for landlords all over the country and what we have seen is that the Possession Claim Online (PCOL) service has really helped landlords with their Section 8 cases. Most of the time, when we upload and file the claims on the court system website, we get hearing dates straight back which is a real bonus.

Unfortunately, I'm also coming across more of what I would term 'sham defences', where the tenant is simply trying to delay eviction. If a tenant decides to file a defence on the day of the hearing, it's difficult for the judge to ignore them and grant a possession order, so they adjourn the case, asking for more evidence. Delaying tactics like this can result in tenants being able to stay in your property for an additional three or four months after the initial court hearing.

And while you have to pay for legal advice, your tenants can secure it for free from the Housing Possession Court Duty scheme! So bear in mind that they might be just as informed as you are about the process,

The first thing I do before recommending court action for landlords is to check that they're 'squeaky clean'. The majority of tenants do not turn up to court to defend the case but if they do, most defences are:

- maintenance repair issues at the property
- the landlord has not protected the tenant's deposit
- they are waiting for housing benefit to be paid
- they dispute the rent arrears
- the landlord has been harassing them.

At most courts nowadays, there is a duty solicitor who will give free advice to the tenant and if the tenant feels they have a defence they should quite rightly argue their case. But some tenants will try to play the court system, using delaying tactics to stay in the property longer.

Remember: These hearings are listed for just five minutes, and there are lots of these hearings at court which puts you under pressure for time, so if the judge feels the arguments and evidence cannot be dealt with in that time, the case will be adjourned… which will unfortunately cause you delays, resulting in extra legal fees and lost rent.

Come court day, it's advisable that you – and your letting agent, if you use one – are there to demonstrate that you care about the case and that securing possession really matters to you. It also means that if the judge asks any questions or the tenant makes any 'new' accusations, you can answer them right away, hopefully preventing the judge from adjourning the case to a later date.

If you decide to employ us, we will run the court case on your behalf and take away the strain.

The courts can make some decisions there and then. For example, if we're evicting the tenant through a Section 8 Notice and use mandatory grounds, as long as we can prove the case without doubt, the court will grant possession and a money order if the tenant is in arrears.

If you get the possession, that doesn't mean you get your property or money straight away – if only it were that simple! Possession for the property normally takes 14 days to be granted by the courts and, if the tenant still refuses to leave, it can take weeks to gain possession via a bailiff.

You should also be aware that if your tenant is considered to be suffering from financial hardship, the court can extend the possession order to up to 42 days (six weeks).

Key steps

It's vital that you're well prepared when you go to court.

1. **Both you and the tenant should have copies of the court papers**

2. **Read the copies of the 'claim of possession' and the 'defence form'**

3. **Make sure you turn up on the correct date!**
   Dress smartly for court, prepare yourself mentally and answer all questions honestly. You may be angry with the tenant, but try not to show it. In some cases the whole thing is over and done within a matter of minutes.

4. **The court makes a decision on the case**

5. **Once the evidence is heard, the court will do one of the following:**

- Dismiss the case altogether due to failure of procedure, wrong paperwork or because the tenant has made up the rent arrears
- Delay the case due to lack of evidence
- Legally decide on what happens next.

5. Possession order is granted
If the judge agrees with your case, they will grant an 'order for possession', which means you can have your property back after the time period set by the court and the time it takes to get a bailiff to evict the tenant.

Who to work with

Being in court can be quite daunting if you're doing it for the first time and, with the delaying tactics increasingly being used by tenants, I'd strongly recommend you use a professional eviction company or a solicitor who's used to handling these kinds of cases.

The cost of using a professional company, such as Landlord Action, is tiny in comparison to the amount it could cost you in time and hassle if you try to do it all yourself and potentially get it wrong.

Questions to ask

If you're going to court, you must understand both your own case and any defence the tenant may be putting forward:

1. On what grounds are you taking the tenant to court?
2. What are the key pieces of evidence you're putting forward?
3. What, if any, defence can the tenant claim – especially at the last minute? (eg maintenance and repairs you might not have carried out or safety certificates not up to date.)

4. Think through or ask your legal advisers what questions might be raised that you'll have to answer.
5. Find out what the result of the court case is likely to be.

Understand that, even if you win in court, this doesn't mean you get your property or money back straight away. It can take time to evict the tenant and you may never see a penny of the lost rent or damage costs.

••

Hot Tip

AVOID COURT, IF POSSIBLE. If you can find an amicable solution prior to going to court, it's cheaper, less hassle and saves fellow taxpayers a lot of money!

CHAPTER 47
WHAT TO DO WHEN THE DECISION IS IN YOUR FAVOUR AND THE TENANT STILL DOESN'T PAY

Tenants sometimes pay up eventually – even several years after the court case – in order to get their County Court Judgment (CCJ) removed.

There's nothing more frustrating than going to the effort of mounting a legal case against a tenant, winning it in court, then finding out this means very little, in reality.

The best you should hope for is that you'll eventually get your property back. In some cases, you may get back the rent arrears and money for any damages as well.

I have had a number of cases where a claim has been made against a tenant for monies owed, but they've simply disappeared without paying up. In this case, a County Court Judgment would be put on their credit record.

CCJs are not automatic in all cases of arrears; landlords have to apply to the court to get the money order enforced in this way. However, it is worth making the effort, even if you don't get your money straight away, as a ruling in your favour has very negative implications for a tenant.

A County Court Judgment (CCJ) remains on somebody's record for six years. If a tenant has a CCJ against them, securing another tenancy, loan finance, a mortgage, a credit card, a mobile phone – and, in some cases, even insurance – is really difficult for them, and will certainly cost a lot more money. This hassle and expense mean they often eventually pay you what you're owed, to get the CCJ removed so they can get on with their lives.

I am planning to campaign to the Ministry of Justice to get CCJs issued automatically to tenants where their landlord has been to court on a Section 8 possession claim hearing and been awarded arrears.

This would be helpful for the tenants' future prospective landlords, as it would show up on their referencing for any new properties they look to rent after being evicted. As it stands, landlords are not warned that an applicant has been evicted for rent arrears and could be a serial bad tenant.

The problem we see at Landlord Action is that landlords don't want to spend the money on trying to enforce the money order and turn it into a CCJ because they don't want to throw good money after bad, especially as they know the tenant may have numerous other debts and creditors chasing them. But this debt lasts for six years and remember a lot of tenants aspire to own their own property one day; if their credit rating is affected, especially by a CCJ, they will need to pay you the debt back and have the CCJ satisfied so they can repair their credit rating and get a mortgage.

Once you've won in court, there are several ways of securing the money you're owed, depending on the tenant's personal circumstances.

Try to enforce the judgement
Either we or the court's bailiffs can help you try to collect money owed from the tenant. Bailiffs secure money via a 'warrant of execution' – a straightforward, one-page form, which states your claim (or you could request the money yourself online via moneyclaim.gov.uk) and asks the tenant to pay what they owe within seven days. If this doesn't happen, the bailiff can enter wherever the tenant is living and, as long as the possessions are theirs, take goods to the value of the debt so they can be sold off to raise the funds you're owed.

Sometimes using a county court bailiff can produce negative results, as I feel they are overworked and underpaid and not incentivised to collect debts. So an alternative is using High Court Sheriffs, where you arrange to transfer the case to the High Court from the county court (which you can do as long as the debt is more than £600), and they will visit the debtor to collect the money owed, adding their fees onto the debt for the debtor to pay.

Secure money from the tenant's wages
If the tenant is employed, you may be able to have the court's money order request sent to the tenant's employer, so the money can be deducted directly from their wages.

Freezing of the tenant's bank account
You request a bank or building society to stop any money going out of the tenant's account until you're paid the money you're owed.

Put a charge on any land or property the tenant owns
If the tenant has been renting from you but actually owns a property themselves, it may be possible to put a charge on that property so they can't sell it until you have been paid back the money you're owed.

In order to work out which enforcement it's best to pursue, you need to look at the tenant's circumstances. Where they are living? Are they working? Do they have a bank account? If the answer to these is yes, then it may be best to apply to have the money deducted from their wages, or to have their bank account frozen until you're paid.

If they aren't working or don't have the money, but do have other assets, such as a car or a motorbike, bailiffs can seize these assets to help pay the debt. In the biggest debt case we were involved with, we seized an Aston Martin! If they own property or land but have no cash or belongings, we can put a charge order on their property. If they appear to have nothing, we can serve a bankruptcy demand, making their on-going life more difficult, which may give them the incentive they need to pay up.

You need to be aware that it's even more costly to carry out enforcement notices than it is to go to court. Costs tend to vary between £300 and £600, rising to nearly £1,000 if we end up putting a charge on someone's property.

You need to work out – and this is something we can help with – which course of action is most likely to persuade the tenant to pay the money they owe you and whether it's financially worthwhile pursuing them.

Key steps

1. **Find out your options**
   Speak to the court to clarify what options are open to you to enforce their decision.

2. **Work out the best way to motivate the tenant to pay**

3. **Pursue the claim**
   Progress the debt claim paperwork and start chasing the tenant.

   At Landlord Action we have a debt recovery department specialising in collecting rent for landlords from tenants and we offer fixed fees for this service.

   Getting money from the tenant can be a tough task – you have to be patient and allow time for the legals to be effected.

Who to work with

We can help you secure rent arrears following a successful court case, as can many other companies, and even the court bailiffs will be able to assist you. If you have some form of insurance for loss of rent, then speak to your insurance company, as they may advise you on who to use, or they may pursue the tenant themselves.

Some companies will offer a 'no win, no fee' and others, like us, will offer a fixed fee so you know exactly what to budget for.

Make sure that any company you use really knows what they're doing and has experience in collecting rent from residential tenants. They also need to understand the money order that has been granted and the tenant's circumstances, so they collect the debt in a way that gives you the best chance of being paid.

Questions to ask

When working with a company to collect debts from a tenant, you need to be sure they're experienced at what they do.

1. Do they abide by the OFT guidelines for debt collection companies?
2. Do they have experience of collecting arrears from private residential tenants?
3. Can they give you names of past landlord clients for references?
4. Do they offer a 'no collection, no fee' or 'fixed fee' service?
5. Review their terms of business, understand their cost structure and know what you will be paid.
6. Can they put a bad credit rating on the tenant?
7. Do they have their own debt collectors or do they outsource the work to other people?
8. What processes do they use to collect rent from tenants?
9. Can they chase tenants who have gone abroad?
10. What happens if the debt isn't collected?
11. Make sure they don't charge up-front fees and if the fees are fixed, always get a breakdown.

••

Hot Tip

USE A BAILIFF. Don't ever turn up at the tenant's home yourself to demand payment or try to seize their belongings. This must always be done legally, through a bailiff.

Case Study

When you go to court on a Section 8 hearing, the judge will order possession and that the tenant has to pay – normally within 14 days. If they fail to do so, then you have to enforce the monies; only then does it become a registered County Court Judgment. It is not deemed as a CCJ until you enforce, then it will show on a tenant's future credit score.

The biggest rent recovery case we have had at Landlord Action was £90k including High Court enforcement fees, where we instructed a High Court Sheriff company to transfer the County Court Judgment up to a High Court Writ. They managed to seize an Aston Martin car. The debtor agreed to pay the debt in full over three instalments.

But it is a real rarity that your tenant will have an Aston Martin as an asset and even rarer that it would be free of finance.

CHAPTER 48
SECURING RENT FROM A TENANT THAT HAS LEFT

On average, landlords are owed approximately £5k in arrears from their tenants. Even though a tenant has left your property, you can still pursue them for money owed. (Source: Landlord Action)

If your tenant has moved out – even if they've escaped abroad – it doesn't mean you can't pursue them for the rent they owe you.

First, you need to double check and be sure you know your tenant has abandoned the property, and is not just avoiding you because they owe you rent, or simply gone on holiday. If you believe the property has been abandoned, speak to the neighbours to find out if they have seen the tenant recently.

The first thing you need to do is find the address at which the tenant is now living. Without this information, you can't apply to the courts to get your money back, so find all the referencing information you took on the tenant before they moved in. If it was done properly, they should have supplied you (or your agent) with lots of useful information that you can use to trace them, such as their full name and date of birth.

Talk to their original personal and work references to see if they know where the tenant is currently living, and it may even be worth contacting the tenancy deposit scheme you used to see if they can help with forwarding details for the deposit. You should certainly alert them to the fact that the tenant has absconded without paying!

Do you have a next of kin or parent's address from when you carried out the referencing?

Things like social media can be incredibly helpful. Surprisingly, regardless of how much trouble they're in, people tend to keep their Facebook profiles going! And speak to the neighbours, as the tenant may have inadvertently shared information that might be useful to you.

If you're struggling to find the tenant yourself, Landlord Action (or other companies) can try to trace them. Some companies do this using technology and databases, such as the Electoral Roll, while others, including us, have expert trace agents. To help us, we'll need as much information about the tenant as possible.

If we're able to recover the money for you, we'll keep it in a client protected account and pass it on to you as possible.

Key steps

1. **Find out where the tenant currently lives. If not known, you may need to instruct a tracing agent**

2. **Be sure what assets they have**
    Find out how much money or what belongings the tenant has that will make up what they owe you. You don't want to throw good money after bad if there is no realistic way of collecting.

3. **Contact the tenant, in writing**
    Send formal letters to the tenant, advising them of what they owe you, and keep copies.

4. **Keep track of the tenant in case they move again**

5. **Take the tenant to court**

If they don't pay what they owe you, take them to court and secure a CCJ.

Who to work with

You should be able to find the tenant from your own referencing details. If not, you can work with any of the following types of companies. Some will just find the tenant for you; others, such as Landlord Action, will do everything, from start to finish.

1. Online facility, which can access various databases

2. Specific rent recovery agency (such as Landlord Action)

3. Tracing agent

4. Private detective

Make sure the company you use is experienced in tracing and securing rent from tenants, both legally and in a way that motivates the tenant to pay you what they owe. Landlord Action offers a fixed-fee tracing service: www. landlordaction.co.uk/debt-recovery/residential-debt-recovery/

Questions to ask

The main questions you need to ask a tracing and rent arrears company are:

1. What experience do they have in tracing residential tenants?
2. How long does it normally take to find a tenant?
3. If they don't find the tenant, do you still have to pay them?
4. Will they chase the tenant for arrears?

5. Can they offer the tenant instalment payments?
6. How do they keep track of the tenant once found?
7. Once the money has been secured from the tenant, will the company keep it in a protected client account?
8. How long will it take to send the money on to you?
9. Can they take the tenant to court?
10. Are they aware of the right notices and forms that need to be completed for your specific case?

• •
Hot Tip

IS IT WORTH IT? Make sure you weigh up whether it's really worth the hassle and cost of tracing and securing the money from the tenant.

CHAPTER 49
WHO TO ADVISE OF YOUR BAD TENANT EXPERIENCE

As you know, I regularly appear on the Channel 5 show, Bad Tenants, Rogue Landlords. If you are currently going through a live eviction case, and wish to tell your story to other landlords to help educate them, please feel free to contact us at Landlord Action and maybe you could feature in a future programme.

When you've put a significant amount of your money into a property so that you can let it to someone as a home, then a tenant comes in and either causes a huge amount of damage or doesn't pay rent – or both – it can be upsetting and stressful. And if you're in this situation, you'll understandably want to tell everyone about it, naming and shaming the tenant to anyone who'll listen.

However, you do have to be careful, as you can be prosecuted for defamation of character, so causing problems for your tenant might ultimately cause you more problems of your own.

The best way to respond to a bad tenant is to take the issue to the court and get a CCJ (County Court Judgment) issued against the tenant's name. All you need is some good legal advice and the tenant's current address.

The CCJ will make it known to any companies carrying out credit checks on the tenant in the future that they've had credit problems in the past.

This means it'll be difficult for the tenant to find a new place to rent, to get a mortgage and to sign up to credit agreements for things like a mobile phone or TV and film packages.

There are also other companies that you can alert about problems you've experienced. Experian have launched a service called Rental Exchange (www.experian.co.uk/rental-exchange/tenants.html), which includes a tenant's rental payment history in credit reports. Good for tenants who pay on time; bad news for tenants who don't.

Also check out landlordreferencing.co.uk, which takes information about tenants who have defaulted and alerts other landlords and letting agents.

Key steps

If your tenant is receiving benefits or you're receiving rent directly from the local authority, they should be the first people you alert that the tenant has absconded. You should also advise companies you worked with on creating the tenancy, anyone who was involved in referencing and the utilities and services to your property that the tenant may also owe money to. Notify:

1. Your letting agent (especially if they only looked after you for tenant find/let)

2. The insurance company and tenancy deposit scheme

3. Utility companies – gas, electricity and water

4. Local authority for the council tax

5. Any other service providers, such as TV and telephone

6. The electoral roll (if they had registered)

7. The company they worked for

8. Anyone who provided references and guarantors

9. Companies who have written to the tenant, whose paperwork the tenant has left behind

10. The credit company you used to reference the tenant

11. Could you have negotiated a deal with the tenant to vacate the property sooner?

Finally, you can advise fellow landlords at local networking events and/or send a brief summary of your case study to newspapers and TV production companies, who may help you find the tenant.

At Landlord Action, we expose serial bad tenants that we know have been evicted on more than one occasion. We will email our database and warn them about these individuals that prey on landlords and we also name them in the press.

Who to work with

In the main, you'll need to alert most of the companies yourself that the tenant has left owing you money. If you have a full management service from your letting agent, they should do much of this work for you.

However, securing the support of a rent arrears company to help ensure you're able to place a CCJ on the tenant's credit record might be worthwhile, if you can afford it.

Questions to ask

Work through where you think the process of assessing, referencing and letting to the tenant went wrong. Try to make sure you know what to do in the future to avoid ending up with a bad tenant again.

1. Could you have protected the tenant's deposit in another way that would have better helped you to find them?

2. What went wrong in the referencing process?

3. Could you have taken more information about the tenant, such as a car registration, that would have helped you trace them?

4. Would more frequent periodic visits have protected the property from being damaged?

5. Were rent arrears caught soon enough?

6. Did you or the company you worked with try to secure the rent arrears quickly enough?

7. Was it foreseeable that tenant would leave the property before you had a chance to ascertain where they might move to next?

8. Would it have saved you money to have paid for loss of rent and legal insurance cover?

9. Should you have secured a guarantor?

10. Did you have an up-to-date tenancy agreement that allowed you to pursue the tenant arrears through the courts?

Hot Tip

PREVENTION IS BETTER THAN CURE! Make sure you carry out thorough due diligence on future tenants, so they know it isn't worth absconding because you'll be able to find them.

CHAPTER 50
SOME FINAL WORDS

Demand is still really strong in the private rental sector. It is estimated by 2039 there will be 74 million people living in the UK. Where are these extra people going to live? When purchasing a property is little more than a dream to many people, there will continue to be a need for quality housing to rent rather than buy.

The private rental sector currently stands at 21% of our total housing sector and is predicted to rise to 24% by 2021, according to agents Knight Frank. There has been a shortage of government-provided housing stock for a number of years and a need for approximately 250,000 properties a year. Currently about 130,000 homes are being provided by Build to Rent, developers and housing associations, which means private landlords will continue to play an important role in bridging the gap.

Knight Frank say £21billion was invested in the private rental sector between 2007 and 2016 and predict that in five years' time the professionally managed PRS will be the third largest asset class in the UK. Buy to let still offers a steady, safe long-term income source, with capital appreciation.

But of course, since writing the first edition of this book in 2015, landlords have faced constant changes and challenges and many have asked me why the government is constantly "meddling" in our sector.

The reason is they want the sector to become more professional, they want landlords to understand their legal responsibilities of renting out a safe property to a tenant, for example understanding that they have to have a valid EPC/gas safety certificate.

The clampdown on rogue landlords and agents is welcomed, but they are still a very small minority, who unfortunately give our industry a bad name.

When I sat on one of these early consultations with the Ministry of Housing, Communities & Local Government (MHCLG), I emphasised the importance of naming and shaming these rogues and said prospective tenants should have access to this information, before paying out any money for a new tenancy.

This will only work with the back-up of tough enforcement but hopefully now that councils can retain the fines they issue of up to £30k this will incentivise them more, especially where there has been a cut to their budgets.

The government's view is tenants are paying more rent than ever before and so should have a property to live in that is worth the money. They do not want tenants being overcharged, which is why deposits will be limited to six weeks, with only one week's holding deposit being only allowed to be taken.

Furthermore, in 2019, Client Money Protection will become mandatory for letting agents to protect the consumer against any misappropriation of rents and deposits and it's expected tenants will not have to pay any fees. In the future, it is becoming quite clear that letting agent regulation is coming and these changes are all good news for landlords as it's likely to help ensure a consistent quality of service from letting agents. I also believe the government will want landlords to be registered with local authorities, as they are in Scotland and Wales, with them also having to become members of a redress scheme.

However, landlords have seen challenges to their business over the last few years.

Housing benefit payments are now moving to the new controversial Universal Credit system which is affecting tenants' ability to pay their rent. The government has said it is getting people off benefits and back into work quicker, which is good, but the result has been rent arrears soaring, and the government having to implement quicker payments.

Secondly, there is the introduction by George Osborne of Section 24 – which has become known as the tenant tax. This will change the way a lot of landlords think about their portfolios, and a large number of landlords who are heavily leveraged on interest-only mortgages are selling their properties as they can no longer benefit from higher rate income tax relief; we are seeing this first hand at Landlord Action.

Thirdly, the introduction of an additional 3% stamp duty on a buy to let purchase, has made small landlords think. Are first-time buyers now snapping up properties landlords are selling (which was the plan) or simply deciding it's still not worth buying versus renting?

Of course, millions of pounds are being made by the Treasury by all of these changes.

One downside to these policies is that some landlords may increase rents and some will evict tenants because they need vacate possession to sell their property, which will only increase homelessness and put further pressure on councils. The long-term plan is that the government wants to encourage long-term tenancies, but so far, few of these policies encourage landlords to 'trust' the system enough to sign up to the current consultation on three-year tenancies.

Just realise you are in business and don't see yourself as an amateur landlord. Even if you have just one property, like the majority of landlords (thought to be over 60%), you need to look at all the various safeguards in renting, from choosing – and doing your due diligence on – suppliers, to educating yourself on the changes, laws and regulations, by joining a landlord association such as the Residential Landlords Association or the National Landlords Association, and by going online and reading updated property news websites such as www.landlordzone.co.uk and many others.

If you're considering self-managing, make sure you have the time to do this and don't forget to put a price on your time, too. If you can't commit many hours to managing your property, then you MUST MUST MUST use a letting agent, as previously mentioned in this book.

Landlording is still a good business, but landlords to have to adapt to the changes in the private rental sector. It's becoming more regulated and the government wants you to become more professional. Supply and demand will dictate.

But despite the challenges, buy to let works for those on long-term plans, in areas of predicted future growth. Remember that in 20 years, our population is predicted to have risen to 74 million. Where are these people going to live? Many of them will need to rent.

Happy Landlording!